PEEBLES

REMEMBERED

Memories of Peebles

*Collected and Edited
by
Susan Stewart, John Rogers,
Marjorie Renton, Margaret Brown and David Beadle*

Members of the Council of the Tweeddale Society

The Tweeddale Society

First published October 2005

ISBN 0-9551108-0-7
978-0-9551108-0-1

Copyright © The Tweeddale Society 2005

Published by The Tweeddale Society, Rathmore, Springhill, Peebles, EH45 9ER

Printed by The Pen-y-Coe Press, 5 and 7 Bridge Street, Penicuik, Lothian, EH26 8LL

Figs. 21 and 22   By kind permission, Crown Copyright: Royal Commission on the Ancient and Historical Monuments of Scotland.

Thanks to the following for providing photographs: David Tait, figs 1, 4, 5, 10, 11 and for cover (adapted); Margaret Jack, figs 6, 13, 14, 19; Bessie Johnstone, figs. 3, 16; John Renwick, fig.17; Ken MacOwan, fig 20; Ilene Brown, fig.2; John Brown, figs, 7, 8, 9; Leonard Grandison, fig 11; Jean Phillips, fig. 15; The Tweeddale Society, figs 12, 18.

Contents

Why and how we made this book	5
The Contributors	5
1. Tweed's Fair River	7
2. Family and Childhood	18
3. Markets, Farming and Forestry	34
4. Peebles at Work	51
5. Leisure and Beltane	67
6. People and Organisations, and hedgehogs	81
7. Peebles at War	98
8. Tourism and Transport	106
9. Growth and Change	114
10. Booklist	124
11. Index	125

The 'Three Fishes of Peebles' coat of arms dates from the twelfth century. The Latin Contra Nando Incrementum which accompanies it can be translated as 'Progress against the Stream'.

Illustrations

1	Fishing on Tweed	8
2	The Wire Bridge and Wire Bridge Cottage	12
3	The Johnstone Family	19
4	Children Playing on Cuddyside	24
5	Peebles High Street as our contributors' parents and grandparents knew it	34
6	Harrowing on Edderston Farm	39
7	Thrashing machine at Bonnington Farm	44
8	Reaper-binder at work at Bonnington Farm	45
9	Milking machine at Bonnington Farm	48
10	Damdale and Damcroft Mills	54
11	The Sand Boat on Tweed	59
12	Members of The Tweeddale Society at Elie, May 1935	71
13	50th Beltane Queen, Margaret Jack, and Court	75
14	Robert Jack, Cornet 1951, leading the Riders past the Old Paris Church	76
15	Guide Commissioner Jean Phillips and Alistair Cummings hold up the light of Guiding at Venlaw	88
16	8th Battalion Royal Scots at Drill Hall, Autumn 1939	99
17	Peebles Section, 'D' Troop, 228 Battery, 66th Medium Regiment Royal Artillery, at Drill Hall, Autumn 1939	100
18	Charabanc	108
19	George Jack with his Milk Cart	109
20	The shop of J. MacOwan, Watchmaker and Jewellery	117
21	The same shop after modernisation	118
22	The Old Fire Station	119

Original engravings © John Rogers on pages 3, 7, 10, 14, 35, 50, 51, 52, 67, 68, 80, 95, 97, 104, 113, 114 and 124.

Why and how we made this book

This collection of memories of Peebles is not the first, nor we are sure the last, to be made with the purpose of preserving for the present and future generations the sights, sounds and experiences of people who lived in Peebles in the twentieth century. Changes have come so fast, and been so profound, as many of the testimonies in this book bear witness, that we felt that we could make a contribution towards preserving them into the twenty-first century. We hope that you will enjoy and value these memories.

Some of the pieces have been written by the contributors themselves. Others were collected orally by us and transcribed from tape recordings. The strict method advised by oral historians is to transcribe and print every nuance of the speaker's words – hesitations, repetitions and deviations all spelled out in the accent and form of the original. We felt that such academic rigour would not be appropriate for this collection, so while we have kept closely and faithfully to the words of those we interviewed, we have, we hope, made their memories read more smoothly on the printed page to let you hear the voices of the different speakers. We have arranged the memories by broad themes, so that recollections of similar experiences can be ready together and compared and contrasted. The same places and the same incidents can be recalled from different perspectives and this makes them all the more fascinating. We have occasionally included items of interest which explain and illustrate what our contributors are telling us, as well as some photographs which they have kindly let us use.

For reasons of length, we have not been able to include all the material collected, though it remains in its original form in our archive of recordings. We are very sorry that we did not have space to include everything but editorial decisions had to be made to achieve an overall balance. If you are disappointed that a favourite memory has not been included, we apologise. We cannot thank you, our contributors, enough – without you the book would not exist.

We are very grateful to the Peebles Common Good Fund and to Dr. John Hooper for their support which has enabled the book to be produced. We thank the Council of the Tweeddale Society and all the members for their support and interest throughout this project. Special appreciation is due to John Rogers for the cover design and the decorative motifs in each chapter; to David Tait for allowing us to choose photographs from his splendid collection and to other contributors who provided photographs; to John MacKay who helped prepare many of the photographs; and to The Pen-y-Coe Press for coping with our inexperience. And finally we thank you, the readers of this book, whose interest and we hope enjoyment of this book will help to keep the past of Peebles remembered.

The Contributors

The list includes the names and a few details of all the contributors. A great deal more can be found out about them in what they tell of their lives in the various sections of the book.

Ilene Brown and **Audrey Edwards** are sisters, born in Galashiels, Audrey on 2 April 1930 and Ilene on 28 June 1932. They came to Peebles as young children and have stayed ever since.

John Brown, born at Bonnington Farm, Peebles, 1939, and lived at and worked Bonnington all his life until retirement in Peebles.
Ian Brunton, born in Peebles 1931. After service in the RAF and working in England, returned to work in Peebles in 1970, where he now enjoys retirement.
Arthur Crittell, born in Peebles, 23 October 1953, where he runs a joinery and glazier business.
Kinnaird Cunningham, born 192^· his family has lived in Hallmanor, Manor Valley, for 100 years. He spent holidays there as a oy and has lived there since 1946.
Sheena Dickson, born in Peebles, October 1922, lived in Peebles all her life except for her years in the ATS during the war.
Willie and Sandy Euman were born in Innerleithen in the 1920s and moved to Peebles in 1932 when they were at primary school.
Pam Fairless, born in Peebles on 23 March 1926, now lives in Peebles after some years in Edinburgh, Stobo and Eddleston.
Peggy Ferguson, born on 24 February 1913, came when a baby to Peebles and has stayed here.
William Goodburn, born in Peebles in 1939, M.A., LLB., W.S., N.P., Hon. Sheriff.
Leonard Grandison, born in Peebles on 4 June 1931. Joined family firm of plastering contractors in 1948 and apart from National Service, involved with running the family business until retirement in Peebles in 1996.
Margaret Jack, born in Peebles in December 1936. Beltane Queen, 1949; Crowning Lady, 1999.
Bessie Johnstone, born in Peebles on 14 April 1914, worked and lived here all her life.
Mary Johnstone, born at Whitebridge, Peebles on 16 May 1920. Lived here all her life.
Sheila Laurie, born in Peebles on 22 October 1916, worked in lawyers' offices in Peebles where she has retired.
Rev. David MacFarlane, Minister of Peebles Old Parish Church, 1970-1997, retired in Peebles.
Ken McOwan, born in Peebles on 27 August 1917, and lived always in Peebles except for his period of service in the RAF from 1936 to 1945.
Sheila Murray, born in Peebles on 12 December 1927. Trained as a teacher and became Assistant Head Teacher, Peebles High School, retiring in 1987 to live in Peebles.
Jean Phillips, District Commissioner for Guides in Peebles 1983-1988, now lives in Peebles.
Dr. Andrew Ramsay, came to Peebles in 1971 to join Dr. Paton's practice and has retired in Peebles.
Carrie Ramsay, born in Peebles on 4 June 1925, lived in Peebles all her life except for her period of service in the special signals unit in the ATS during the war.
James Renwick, born in Peebles on 27 February 1916, lived in Peebles all his life except for service in the Royal Artillery, 1939-45.
Lieutenant-Colonel Aidan Sprot, M.C., J.P., born on 17 June 1919, Lord Lieutenant of Tweeddale 1980-1994, lives at Crookston.
David Tait, born on 14 January 1933, and **Jimmy French,** born on 13 October 1936. Cousins in a long-established Peebles family, life-long friends and, for many years, workmates.
Duncan and Isabel Taylor, born in Peebles in the 1930s. Isabel spent twenty years down south and then came back home to Peebles.
Jean Thomson, born in Peebles on 15 August 1933 and has lived here all her life.

Chapter 1
TWEED'S FAIR RIVER

'Tweed's fair river, broad and deep'.[1]   River Tweed is central to Peebles, both literally and in people's minds and conversation.   *Peggy Ferguson and Mary Johnstone shared their memories:*
Mary: We swam in the Tweed, it was deeper then, you know where the red rock is, that was the Minnies Pool. We called it the Minister's Pool because the Minister stayed in Lea Lodge. We had a diving board on the rock, but, when after the floods the Tweed changed, they took it away because there wasn't any depth.
Peggy: They thought that the Minnies pool was dangerous because there's a terrible amount of rocks.   That was the reason they took the swimming board away because at that time there was that lad that was swept under – it was the current. It was this side of the castle, at the bend of the river. There was a big swimming pool always there.

You used to stand on Tweed Bridge and you saw the salmon going up the Cauld. And there were a lot of poachers. Oh, the poachers! It was hereditary – the Earl of Wemyss – the castle belongs to him. There was a bailiff, but they were well sussed, there was somebody watching. When the whistle went, they were away. Scott – you mind him – he said the bailiff never caught him because he took a bit of pipe with him and if he heard the bailiffs he just submerged – with a pipe in his mouth he was a human submarine, you see, put himself out of the danger zone.
Mary: They climbed trees, oh, you have no idea of the tricks. A lot of campers used to come from Edinburgh and camp at Whitebrig[2] and when it was time for the salmon they said, 'You catch them and we'll come through on a Sunday for them'.   We had a lot in our wash house, you had to hide them because the bailiffs could come after them, yes.
Ian Brunton remembers the excitement of the annual cleanout:
Every August the boys would wait anxiously for the time when the mill dams would be shut down and drained for annual cleaning. There were

---
[1] From 'Marmion" by Sir Walter Scott
[2] Whitebrig or Whitebridge is half a mile outside Peebles on the road to Traquair.   The bridge crosses the Haystoun Burn just before it joins the Tweed

two dams – one ran from the junction of the Tweed and Cuddy to the tail of Tweed Green and the other from where Somerfield's is now to Biggiesknowe. These dams always contained a good stock of trout and eels and when they were drained a free-for-all took place. All the boys, with landing nets made of mutton cloth, fencing wire and a simple wooden handle, had a great and exciting hunt.

Willie and Sandy Euman reminisce about the great days of watching birds and fishing in the Tweed:
Willie: There was a stretch east of Tweed Bridge on the north bank of the river where the sand martins came year after year – there must have been thousands, eh, Sandy? We would stand there and they were flying in and out of their holes while we stood there, under our feet. It was marvellous, everything was just fresh and wonderful, the river itself – the water that was flowing past was almost drinkable, untainted, unspoilt.

Talking of fish, I frequently walk by the river and I have discovered there's hardly any fish left in the Tweed. One never sees a rising trout – it used to be something we all looked forward to – the dinner-hour rise. I did a bit of angling – in fact I did too much angling – I feel a wee bit guilty when I think of all the lovely trout I killed. I still see people and visitors coming with fishing rods and going up the Tweed but what they get, what

Fig. 1   Fishing on Tweed

they're fishing for, I don't know, because I never even see a rising trout any time I'm near the river. I never see the clouds of beautiful duns in great variety which hatched on the bottom of the river, reach the top, fly off, mate and before we know it they were reproducing, landing again in the river, and of course the trout knew about this and they would rise at various times of the day. We would get what we call the dinner-hour rise, and there used to be a surge of people who would stand with a fishing rod and a cast and a fly on the end, a dry fly, with a hook – a dash down to the Tweed to get a go at the dinner-hour rise until it's past, and then we would get the gloaming rise – that's towards the evening. There was rarely a night we weren't out with a fishing rod fishing on the Tweed. The Tweed was running pure and every spring the abundance of fish it gave was unbelievable despite the fact that everybody, yes everybody, nearly everybody I know had a fishing rod. The fishing rods stood at the back door and the line and gut cast was never removed. Usually they'd keep a gut cast with a fly at the end. It was important to try and match the flies that the trout were taking. It was thought the trout, an intelligent creature, could distinguish if the type of fly it was feeding on at the moment wasn't the correct one and you could fish all day with the march brown but if they were taking the blue hen they would never look at your march brown however well it was tied. I myself used to make all my own lures, and I knew where to get all the feathers.

Sheila Laurie remembers both the August cleaning and the poachers:
The Mill Dam was emptied once a year at the Annual Mill Holidays in August. Lots of the young lads would 'guddle' the trout that were left at the clearing. The Dam also had a bridge over it at the end where it went into the Tweed. This was used by poachers of salmon to escape being caught by the bailiffs. Those days men poached to earn a bob or two.

   The Boat Hole was a great place for us. Charlie Hislop hired out a few rowing boats in the summer. He had a whistle and a loud shout – to any youngster who would be standing up capering in the boat! We were terrified of him but we respected him too because he really cared for we children of the Green. Charlie was a 'fisher' and lots of other fishers would be around the Boat Hole when Tweed was in spate and lots of tales would be spun. There was quite a 'Swirl Pool' here also which was very deep. Tweed of course came right into the Banking at this point. There was a 'Cauld' from the Boat Hole side over to the other side of Tweed where we often saw the salmon leaping over it. Unfortunately this has long gone and there are islands in Tweed now that were never there before. I have often seen poachers run the Cauld, climbing over the Dam Bridge and up by the Green to the Old Town to escape the Bailiffs.

Duncan Taylor has some fine tales of how to escape the law:
I knew a local who used to do an awful lot of poaching and a certain policeman in Peebles was always trying to catch him. He was coming along the street on his bike and the policeman spied him with a big parcel under his arm, and he says, 'What have you got in the parcel?' 'Fish.' 'Right. Down to the Polis Office.' And he opens up the parcel and he's got a couple of cods' heads! He'd been along to the fishmonger to get fish to feed the cats at the mill.

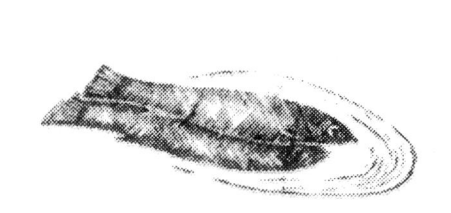

Duncan continues:
When I was twelve or thirteen, we had this new teacher who suggested we went on a nature walk. 'Certainly, Sir!' So we'd go up Cademuir and the Manor and when were up Manor we were away killing salmon! That was the last nature walk we ever got.

   I left school on the Friday and was working on the Monday. I was a plasterer with Grandison's. I was all over the country, all over the place, it was quite a good experience. One day I wasn't working so I went up Manor with the post office van. That day, we killed two or three salmon and coming back down the road, there were the police and the water bailiff. 'Oh what can we do here?' I say. 'No problem,' the postman says, 'You just go in with the mail bags.' He flapped the window shut and drove right through the road block – you can't stop the Royal Mail – and there I was lying in the back under the mail bags with the salmon!

And it wasn't just salmon that were at risk, as Duncan's next story tells. Two of his mates had been duck shooting and were stopped by the police on the way home:
Bert's got the barrel of the shot gun down his trouser leg and wee Scotty got the butt. 'Whose gun is it?' demanded the law. Wee Scotty says, 'It's mine' but Bert says, 'It's not your gun at all,' and that way no one knew whose gun it was. So eventually it was established that it was Bert's gun, and the police were writing all this down. According to their record, Bert says, 'I bought it for thruppence at St. Joseph's jumble sale.'

The sheriff at that time, Isabel Sinclair, she was telling us how everyone was laughing in court. 'Bert,' she says, 'Were they wild ducks?' Well, it's the law – if they were not wild, you can shoot them. 'Were they wild ducks?' 'Well,' says Bert, 'They weren't too pleased!' An extra two pounds for cheek, he got!

Kinnaird Cunningham tells of poachers in Manor Valley:
There have always been poachers in the Manor Water until the last year or two. They were poaching from a whole series of landowners, farmers up the Valley, but I don't think they worry very much. It's the bailiffs that worry because of the fishermen down the river, but there's so few fish come up now and the price of salmon is so low that it's not really worth their while. There used to be gangs from Hamilton, Wishaw and Motherwell that used to come. One day we found a bag in our wood down there – two bags – and one bag had a lot of wet clothes in it and the other bag had thirteen salmon in it. Very fresh. So we told the water bailiff people. It was just before Christmas and we came back from seeing somebody to find the place looking like an army camp, full of people in camouflage uniforms speaking on field telephones and so on and we didn't really quite like to ask what was going on, but we could hear them saying, 'Yes, the car's just coming up now, it's up past, it's turned, it's turned right round....NOW.' They didn't catch them until after they'd picked it up and gone off down the Valley; I think they stopped them down there.

There was quite a lot of poaching in the days when salmon was worth poaching. Now I'm afraid they don't bother much. The locals always took the odd salmon, yes, it was perfectly normal occasionally to find a salmon on the back door step in the morning – somebody had gone out to get a fish and had come back with two, but we didn't ask any questions. You could look out of our bedroom window and see the lights of the poachers up there quite often. Sometimes they got very rough, and one or two people were told 'You just keep quiet – if you tell the police about us we'll be back and we'll do your house,' so hence 'live and let live' to some extent, and if the police caught them somewhere else then that was fine but not many people tried to report them to the police.

Ilene Brown remembers the Wire Bridge ....
The Wire Bridge Cottage was a favourite place. Mr and Mrs Bert Sherriff lived there with their son Albert and daughter Roma. Mr Sherriff was the gardener for Kingsmeadows. There really was a wire bridge and Mr Sherriff had the key. Sometimes we were allowed to cross over to the Kingsmeadows side. It was lovely to walk along and see the Dolls House which is still there. I also remember a bronze deer, but I don't know if it is still there.

Fig. 2 The Wire Bridge and Wire Bridge Cottage.

.... and Aidan Sprot explains why it is no longer there.
At Wire Bridge Cottage, which is down the river just beyond Kerfield Farm, there used to be a private bridge for Kingsmeadows. It was a bridge made of wire. And it was very similar, I understand, to the one at Gattonside down near Melrose. And this one here, Wire Bridge, was destroyed by trees that came down in a flood and carried the bridge away, which is very sad, because it would make a most wonderful walk. You could go completely round. If you started at Wire Bridge, you could cross the river, go right up on mostly Burgh land, right up to the railway viaduct, cross over there and come the whole way back down the other side and you'd virtually be in a park or countryside or a wood the whole way – made a lovely walk. I've always been very much in favour of the Wire Bridge being rebuilt but it's the usual thing – finance.

The Tweed and Cuddy in flood was a regular occurrence, as Dr Andrew Ramsay remembers:
The Memorial Hospital on Tweed Green was at risk from flooding from the river. On either side of the outside doors of the nursing home you can still see the slots into which sheets of iron with rubber padding were put to stop the river flooding into the hospital. They were not always successful and at flood times matron had been observed in Wellington boots with her skirts

caught up, carrying on despite the incoming water. In 1963 one of my colleagues well remembers obtaining help from police and firemen to carry patients upstairs, and there were rowing boats on the putting green.

Jean Thomson has good reason to remember her first day at work:
I started work in 1948. I started work on the Monday and actually I wasn't fifteen till the following Sunday. But with me being left school, because my birthday was before the school started again, so I started work when I was fourteen but officially it was fifteen. And that Friday, which was 13th August, I was sent round to what we called the bureau – the employment exchange at the top of Damdale – it's a small house now, on the corner, it used to be an optician – and I was sent round there about something about starting work. Now, that night before, during the Thursday, there was really heavy rain and the Cuddy actually flooded Damdale Mill which was where Damcroft is now. There was the mill dam that led into Damdale Mill that provided the power to Thorburn's Mill[3] and the river had risen so much that the Mill across there was all under water, and I remember bales of cloth being brought up from the warehouse to try to spread them out to see if they could dry or do anything with them, and all the houses down Cuddyside were all flooded too, and in Dovecot going down to work that morning there was a mark, more or less where the old railway line used to be[4] and that was where the river had been up to during the night. This was in August – Friday 13th! And the Tweed of course was big too. And all the houses in Tweed Avenue were flooded and the bottom floor of the nursing home was flooded. In fact that happened again, I don't know if it was the following February or maybe a year after that, but that happened again. And it also happened I remember in October, because my cousin – she was having her first baby – and they had to evacuate them all early – of course they stayed in long then – from the nursing home in Tweed Green where all the babies in Peebles used to be born.

William Boyd, a jobbing gardener who lived in Northgate, kept a complete daily record of his working year and his diary for 1949 has survived.[5] Two entries are relevant here:

January 7th: Heavy showers of rain with high wind all day. Cuddy river overflows and houses flooded. It is only a few months ago since the heavy flooding on the night of 12th August which was the worst in memory.

---

[3] For more about mills, see Chapter 4
[4] For more about the railway, see Chapter 8
[5] Our thanks to Mary Hudson for sharing this diary with us.

October 26th: Have had heavy flooding after yesterday's rain and last night's gale and heavy rain. Cuddy and Tweed heavy but not so bad as year ago. Waterside folk had to leave their houses being flooded.

For Peggy and Mary, floods were a normal part of life:
Mary: The Cuddy Brae Lane was always flooded, until they took the water away for Edinburgh. The flood...
Peggy: ...it was at the bottom of the East Brae – Port Brae, Tweed Brae and School Brae – the water was that bad right over the Greens. I've seen it over the Kingsmeadow Road.
From remembering floods, it was only a step to recollecting past winters.
Mary: Then we went sledging.
Peggy: We could do it in the park, a bit of the golf course, or the old golf course up Edderston Road. And we went to Connor Street, when there was snow. We used to go sledging when we were at school. And from the mill – we were going idle quite a bit – we got a huge great sledge, it took four or five. There were an awful lot of whin bushes on the hill and after heavy snowfalls, the sledge would go right through the whin bushes – you got your gloves soaking.
Mary: Mind the train was snowed in at Leadburn and at Cardrona. All you could see was the funnel of the train. It was 14 feet at Horsburgh Castle and it was here for weeks.
Sheila Murray recollects:
Winters were more severe in our young days. Every winter there would be at least one heavy snow fall of several feet and roads would be blocked. Plumbers were kept busy coping with frozen and burst pipes and we had frosts severe enough to freeze Tweed. We used to skate on the curling pond down Kingsmeadow Road.

Hard winters were felt more up Manor Valley than in the town itself, as Sheila Laurie recalls:
We had moved to Manor and were there during the war years. I cycled up and down nearly 12 miles a day to work or many a time walking it when the roads were snow-covered. We had some dreadful winters in the war years.[6] One I recall – the School was shut for six weeks because of blocked roads. Another time I remember my parents had taken a sledge as far as the wee Post Office, one and a half miles approximately – the Saturday bus had managed that far. They took it to Peebles, shopped and I joined them to get home for the weekend. It was to leave Peebles at 1 p.m. By this time word had come through that it was dreadful up the valley again – bus cancelled! We went to see if we could get a car and fortunately there was a Manor lad there who had his car. We knew him although he didn't stay as far up the valley as we were, but of course we knew him well. That lad's name was Charlie and he tried repeatedly to get his car up over this steep hill and corner but it kept sliding back. We ended up getting out into a bitter, bitter, blinding, freezing wind, hail and you name it. We still had over one and a half miles and we really thought we would never get home. Never was the comfort of the oil lamp and coal fire appreciated so much – them were the days!

Kinnaird Cunningham also remembers hard winters in Manor:
Winters were much colder, lasted long, we would reckon that you could see snow up on that bit of hill there until end of April anyway. Now we're lucky to see snow there for two days in the winter. It was distinctly cold in those days. We would get up in the morning and get our shirt, vest and pants out from under the bedclothes where we'd been keeping them warm, and our socks usually, and put them on before we got out of bed, and then hasten into all the other clothes we could lay our hands on. No central heating so we would come into the drawing room in the evening and there was a chair by the door where you put all your coats, and then when you went from the drawing room into the kitchen or somewhere else, you put your coat back on. It was genuinely cold, I think, quite a difference.

   A lot of the winter was spent cutting down trees, cutting up trees, carrying trees in on our shoulders. Now we just take a machine up and bring them down, but it was all cross cut with a cross cut saw – no chain saws – cross cut saws, split with an old felling axe, and that was practically all the heat we had. Mother did have coal for special occasions if somebody was coming to stay, but otherwise we just survived on the wood we could carry on our shoulders – hard work – I don't know how we did it, actually. It got

---
[6] For more about Peebles in the war years, see chapter 8.

us warm several times – cutting it, carrying it in, splitting it and then burning it. But we never got very warm.

I don't know if the summers were warmer or colder. I don't think I marked it down as any great difference between summers now and summers then. It always seemed nice but that's because you remember the days when you went for picnics and forgot the days when you were immured in the house or sent out in the rain to cut wood.

This road, it's been tarred since before the war certainly. We had a slight mess around in the road when they put in pipes down from Megget to Edinburgh – they were huge pipes just below the road here that went straight down the valley.[7] I only once had trouble with snow then because they had a mammoth snowplough called Tinkerbell which used to go racing up and down the valley whenever there was a sign of snow so that they wouldn't get held up with their work. The only time I think it went wrong was when Tinkerbell was up the Valley and the driver was in Peebles and it snowed and the crew couldn't come to get together, but Tinkerbell was very useful in the snow.

Aidan Sprot had his own way of coping with snow:
The best insurance policy I ever took out was to buy a snow plough for the tractor – it's never been used! It sits up in the stackyard and we twice here have been snowed in purely because in these valleys we get very strong winds. I don't know why they made the entrance road from the public road dead straight across the valley with dykes both sides, but these two years we were snowed up, we had a blizzard with the wind that way so you had that much snow drifting. And then the wind went round to the north and came down so we had it solid across so we had to use the two fields to get out because you couldn't snowplough between the dykes because you'd push the dykes down.

William Boyd recorded the extremes of climate in his diary of 1949. The ups and downs of the weather in the first half of the year sound very familiar:
January 1st: Slight fall of snow, hard frost now setting in.
January 2nd: Another slight fall of snow with frost getting severer.
January 3rd: 22 degrees frost[8], very cold day, roads very bad.
January 4th: Still hard frost, 20 degrees.

---
[7] The tunnel from Manor Valley through to the new Megget Reservoir was started in 1978. The pipeline through Manor Valley was laid from March to October, 1981, after the completion of the tunnel.
[8] 10 degrees Fahrenheit or - 12 degrees Celcius

January 5th: A change today, not so cold wind gets up and more like to be some rain.

January 6th: Frost gives way, some rain and much milder now. Snow cleared off roads.

February 6th: Hard frost with nice sunshine, very good day.

February 26th: Had showers of snow last night and hills white today. Very cold wind but keeps fair. Very high winds last night. February goes out with gale winds and heavy showers of sleet. Snow on hills.

March 19th: Nice sunshine today, had frost in morning. Have had a lot of cold winds all week but milder at the end of the week.

April 8th: Hills have a covering of snow last night. Nice day with cold wind about.

April 16th: Lovely day, warm. Having the best days to be remembered in April.

April 17th: A lovely day. Having had 3 or 4 days around Easter being a record, the best that can be remembered, very warm being over 80 degrees[9] in some places.

June 5th: Dry with very cold wind. Had some sunshine. Had heavy rain during last night, high wind, much cooler again. Not very good growing weather owing to the cold winds.

June 6th: Gale wind does a lot of damage to berry bushes and bedding plants. Ground drying very badly, not good for growth.

June 19th: Nice sunny day. A fine spell of weather for cleaning up walks and dirty corners.

---

[9] More than 26 degrees Celcius

Chapter 2
FAMILY AND CHILDHOOD

Now, having set the scene and the climate of Peebles, we turn to the stories of its people. First and foremost, the importance of being born in the right place! Dr. Andrew Ramsay, when he joined the medical practice in Peebles in the 1960s, quickly came to understand the importance of exactly where you were born:

The tradition strongly remains with Peebleans that babies should be born in Peebles if possible because expectant mothers want their child to be a 'gutterbluid'[1] rather than the opposite – 'stourie-fit', which means literally 'dusty-foot' – that is, someone not born in Peebles. This results these days in some last minute dashes to the maternity ward with births in the ambulance en route.

Pam Fairless's story begins nearly eighty years ago:

I was born in Peebles on 23 March 1926, down in the nursing home which overlooks Tweed Green. I think babies were either born there or at home. And then I went home to Eliots Park which was a new scheme that was built after the First World War. My mother and father were married after the First World War. My father was born in a house up in Rosetta Road, Hawthorn Cottage, and my mother was born in Jean Cottage in Dean Park. My grandfather built the houses there and all the family were born there in Jean Cottage, although it's not called Jean Cottage now. He had a carrier business in the town and he had a horse and cart and delivered things to Dalkeith and Eskbank and places like that. And my mother had three sisters and a brother, and my father had just one brother. My grandfather bought this house in 1902 so we have lived in it for over a hundred years. My great-grandmother died in this house and my grandmother died in this house and my father died in this house, so I'm hoping this is where I'll be when I conk out as well.

Yes, it's a real family house and the same except that we have added a bit on at the back. I've put a little stained glass window, not with any writing on it – it's a heart with a Rennie MacIntosh rose – I've put it in the lintel of what was once the back door just to commemorate the fact the family had been in this house for a hundred years.

---

[1] Gutterbluid status can only be claimed by those actually born in Peebles itself, a problem for mothers today when there are no maternity facilities in the town.

Ian Brunton has traced his family's association with the Burgh:
I was born in Peebles in 1931 into the ninth generation of my family who have lived in our Royal and Ancient Burgh. The original Bruntons as far as I can find from my research came to Peebles in the late 1600s from East Lothian.

My 'four-greats' grandmother shared in the family's long association with the armed forces of the Crown. She was born in Dunkirk in 1793 where her father was engaged in the siege of that town during the French Revolutionary War. She returned to live in Peebles and was the oldest inhabitant when she died here in 1888.

Many of the people we interviewed were born in Peebles, like Pam and Ian, and can claim 'gutter-bluid' status, as can Bessie Johnstone:
I was born in March Street on 14 April 1914, and I had an older brother who was eight years older and a younger brother who was five years younger, and I was brought up in the house just opposite the mill gates in March Street, with my maternal grandmother and an uncle all in the one house. My mother's family came from Cambusbarn near Stirling. My dad was one of fourteen – there were ten boys and he must have been the eighth boy, and they needed names for them. My father was called after Dr. Gunn[2] - he was Clement Gunn and my nephew is Clement Gunn Campbell Johnstone. The photograph of them all must have been the Golden Wedding of my grandparents.

Fig. 3 Bessie's grandfather and grandmother surrounded by their fourteen children. Newton and Bessie's father are sitting in front.

Back row: Robert, Isabel, John, William, George, Jessie, Andrew. Middle row: Sandy, Margaret, Norman, Rachel, James.

---
[2] For more about Dr. Gunn, see page 81.

There was Robert, and John, William, George and Andrew – Andrew's still a family name because my grandfather was Andrew – there was Alexander – he was Sandy – Uncle Jamie, he went to New Zealand before the War because at Christmas there was always a sheep sent across for the family. My father was Clement. Uncle Newt, he was badly wounded in the War. His son still stays in Graham Street, he's Newt too and one of my youngest cousins, and Norman, another family name. The four girls were Isabella, called Sis, Janet, called Jessie, Margaret and Rachel, named for her mother.

Arthur Crittell's mother, like Bessie's, settled into a Peebles family:
I was born in the War Memorial hospital, 23 October 1953, born and bred. My grandmother, Annie, on my dad's side, she was born in Eastgate as was her mother. My father's side of the family had generations in Peebles, my mother came from Cumbria, so that side of my family is English. My mother is very much into the way of Peeblesshire and Peebles and the Beltane[3].

Jean Thomson's earliest and very detailed memories are from the 1930s:
My earliest memory of Peebles is when I was two years old. I was actually born in Peebles at Morelands Nursing Home on Tweed Green, but my parents stayed in Innerleithen until my dad came up to work in Ballantynes Mill in Peebles and that was when we moved to Elcho Street. And I can actually remember the day we moved up to Elcho Street. I can remember sitting in one of the big chairs which had been taken off the lorry coming from Innerleithen, and I was sitting on it on the pavement waiting for it to be carried upstairs. Elcho Street is the same as it was then. The only difference is that some of the houses – we were in 21 – now have railings in front, which we didn't have. It was only the downstairs at the end of the block that had the railings round.

I remember going into Renwick's the grocers[4] and seeing an advert for Fairy Soap and the picture was the five quins – the Dionne quins – and that was my earliest memory of Peebles, when I was two. I remember that because I had my third birthday in Elcho Street and because we had cousins coming to stay (their mum had died), my dad bought a bigger house in George Street, and we sold Elcho Street for £290, this would be 1937, and the house they bought in George Street was £320.

---

[3] See chapter 5.
[4] For more about Renwick's the grocer, see chapter 9.

Sheila Laurie recalls happy childhood years at Greenside:
I was born in October 1916 at Greenside, the fifth child of my parents James and Jean Laurie. I had one younger brother, six years between us.

Our house was a very commodious home for a lively family, with two public rooms, three bedrooms and box room, bathroom, kitchenette, plenty of cupboards and gardens back and front. It has gas lighting and coal fires. We had a happy Christian upbringing, not a lot of money but plenty of love. Mother was an extremely clever woman with her hands and made all our clothes up till we were teenagers. I recall her sitting knitting – brown frocks for my sister and me – she trimmed them with rabbit fur! We also had little knitted hats to match! These we received on Christmas morning along with our stocking – one apple, one orange, one new penny, a pair of tin scales, two small glass bottles with scented sweets, a few other pieces I can't quite recall. All were amazing presents from Santa. Our wants were easily satisfied in those days.

Sheena Dickson recalls the importance of her mother's role in the home:
My mother did everything in the house – in those days that was more or less all the mother did. My mother got up in the morning, she made the breakfast, then I'd go to school, and when I came back, she'd made the dinner, go to school again, come back, she'd maybe done some shopping herself in the afternoon and when I came back at 4 o'clock she might ask me to go to a certain shop – we'd need some sugar or we'd need some butter – then I'd come back and it was teatime. I used to help my mother on washing day. Behind the house was just a small building – it had two tubs in it. You had to light the fire in the morning to heat the water, then I used to go up there and help her. There was the scrubbing board, and the sink, and then there was the wringer in between and I used to stand on a stone there to help her. Then the clothes got hung out and afterwards when they were dry you used a mangle – it's like two rollers. Sometimes I helped mother with the shopping but I never did any cooking.

My father would give mother so much for house-keeping for a month but she used to spend it and as a joke she used to turn out her purse at the end of the week and there was nothing in it and he had to end up giving it her every week. In those days that's all the women did, the men paid everything else. Coal was part of my father's salary. My mother would put out the pails in the morning and the man who looked after the furnace at the mill came and filled them up with coal and brought them back to the house. We lived in the kitchen which had a big range and on either side was a cooker.

Pam Fairless remembers the pleasure of being sent down to the local shop:
The first shop I was allowed to visit on my own was Harvey's. This because of the happy chance that there was no break in the pavement from Eliots Park to the foot of Kirkland Street where the shop was situated. Children were often sent for the messages, usually with a written line.

The two Miss Burnetts had the shop at the top of March Street but lived in Wemyss Place. There were sisters but not a bit alike. One was stout and cheery with a deepish voice while the other was thin, wore gold-rimmed spectacles and had a high pitched voice. They both had their hair tightly drawn into a bun and wore spotless white-bibbed aprons. They had a nice bright shop which sold groceries and sweets. In the window facing March Street, a high shelf had a row of big jars of sweets but at the foot, at child level, sat the serviettes in two rows which displayed all the sweets we could buy for a halfpenny or a penny. I and my friends spent many happy times choosing at that window – sometimes even with imaginary money to spend. Thus children entered Burnetts with their minds made up – which was good as the thin Miss B. was not too patient with us. Pointed paper pokes made out of the shiny printed pages of a magazine were used as bags. The sweets we bought were carefully counted and dropped in.

The shop counter was facing at right angles to the window. Behind it were lots of little drawers. In these were kept flour, rice, tapioca and such things which were all sold loose in those days. Big shiny brass scales stood on the counter with different sized weights, and I loved to watch Miss Burnett with the little brass scoop she used, carefully shaking on a little at a time until the two pans balanced. Once balanced, the bag, brown in colour, was neatly folded over and the corners turned in. Miles must have been covered as the Miss Burnetts went back and forth getting each item on our list and putting it tidily with the others on the counter. Then, with a pencil, the price was put beside each item in the list and the total added up. Shopping was slow but pleasurable, as I look back. Waiting our turn did not make us impatient. Watching Miss Burnett was an entertainment and all the waiting customers chatted as we all knew one another in those days.[5]

Pam Fairless's mother used to make her clothes:
She used to send away for a big book of Patterns, to Pontings in London, and this big book came back and I got to choose what material I wanted and the book was sent back with the order. And then she would make my clothes on the sewing machine. Even during the war we wore white for tennis and she even made me a white pleated skirt with a little top to go with it for tennis. And my mother wasn't a hairdresser but she was quite good

[5] There is more about shops in Peebles ....ote - 9.

at making curls with curling tongs, and if there was a party or anything, my friends came to our house and my mother put a chair in the middle of the kitchen and put the tongs on the cooker to heat them and then she gave everybody little curls. We did have a help in the house at one time, but my mother really did everything. Monday was washing day. We had a mangle I can remember when I was young, but we didn't have a copper. But when I was first married, I lived in a flat in March Street and we had a wash house but it was never used. But the copper in the wash house next door was used and this Mrs Wild, her husband was in charge of the Salvation Army here, she got up at three or four in the morning to get the water and the fire lit under and when we got up in the morning Mrs Wild's washing was out on the green.

The making, washing and drying of the family clothes occupied a lot of a mother's time, as first Bessie Johnstone, then Peggy Ferguson and Mary Johnstone remember:

My grandmother made my clothes and my mother knitted. Washing day was in the outside washing house and the copper was always set on the Sunday night for the Monday morning. There were four houses in the block and my mother and her family - I don't know whether she had been the longest there – but she had Monday morning when the copper was set. On Sunday we used to have a bath in the double sink in the washing house, because the water was hot. And then it was always cleaned out and prepared for the family who had it the next day.

Peggy: We were lucky down at Whitebrig, we'd wash in the outside wash house.

Mary: They had the well outside and water had to be carried to the copper and the fire got going to heat the water.

Peggy: Saying that, there were 12 houses down there and two wash houses. It was six and six and they all had a day and you had to stick to your day. Well, we hadn't enough clothes to do out a whole week so my mother had to come down nearly every night doing all our smalls. There were five of us, five girls. Doing all the smalls, to keep us in clean clothes. She did a lot of washing in the house.

And then, of course, the washing had to be dried, as Sheila Murray describes:
Before the days of washing machines, many women had to take their washing to the laundry. They could be seen every Monday morning wheeling their basket of washing, often on a pram, either to the laundry in March Street, or to Greenside Laundry, hanging their clothes to dry afterwards either at Cuddyside, Greenside or Tweed Green next to where the Putting Green used to be.

But Carrie Ramsay tells of disputes about the right to use particular drying greens:

The grounds of Red Lion House go right down to the middle of the water of the Cuddy and there was a great outcry about, 'Oh, they didn't own the fishing in that water,' but they did. And they said, 'There were always drying greens, you know'. Oh no, the drying greens were over the other way, way past, and there wasn't room for drying greens because you went down the bottom of the garden and then there was a wall there, and the mill lade runs through it and between it and the Cuddy there's just this narrow strip of grass, there's no room for anything, but there's a lot of people claiming that the folks shouldn't have it but it belongs to them. There was great discussion about it. And I can remember people coming down from the top of the Northgate to put their washing out on that drying green. The same as is along Tweed Green – there are still poles along Tweed Green on that far path beside the river. The people on Tweed Green have a right to go and hang their washing out today – not a good idea these days![6]

Fig. 4 Children playing on Cuddyside. No room for drying greens here. Washing can be seen drying on Tweed Green on the cover.

---

[6] Isabel Taylor commented that she still maintains her right to use Tweed Green by bringing out odd items from time to time. Duncan also claimed they had a right to graze flocks there and perhaps one day he'll put some sheep there - just for the hell of it!

While mothers dealt with the washing and gossiped and disputed on the drying greens, children were having a variety of experiences in school. Sheena Dickson, born in Peebles in 1922, came back to Peebles when she was six years old:
My grandmother was a teacher and when I came back here she took me to Halyrude School, and I hated it the first day. They made fun of me because I spoke differently, with a different accent from round here. There was one boy who was particularly rude to me. When I stood up to ask a question, he tipped up the seat, and the teacher – she was lovely – said to come out and sit on her knee, but that was the worst thing she could have done because all they did was to shout out 'Teacher's pet, teacher's pet'. Anyway, I got used to them eventually.

So I grew up here and in those days you went to Kingsland School after, and then when you were twelve years old you had an exam and if you passed you could go to the High School. If not you stayed there until you left school. The High School at that time was a fee-paying school and pupils who started at the beginning, their parents were paying, and we went along not paying, so there was some slight animosity to begin with, you know. And we always wore uniform; in the summer time navy-blue gym dress with a cream blouse underneath and a green and yellow sash because Ettrick Forest starts where the High School is – green and yellow are for the forest – and on the dress the badge with PHS for Peebles High School. In the wintertime we wore a black velour hat with green and yellow ribbon and badge and in the summertime we wore a panama hat – it was lovely.

At school in my day up to ten or twelve we printed everything, and it was only when we went to the High School that we started writing. I can still hear one of the teachers saying, 'Up light, down heavy, up light, down heavy' – you know – the copperplate writing with the nibs. At first they wouldn't write when they were new and you had to work at them – you remember the little ink wells?

The teachers were all different characters, some of them I liked, some of them I didn't. Normally it was the one teacher taught you everything but when you went to the High School you had a teacher with maybe an hour of this and an hour of that. I always liked French, I think it was one of my best subjects – I mean I know it's schoolgirl French – I used to get 99% and I thought how can you just get another 1%? And the teacher there, I thought she was French, she would only speak in French in class and would not speak English. In my day if you were going to be in the professions, a teacher or whatever, then you stayed for five years, but I wasn't going to do that, so you just stayed three years. You had this exam for your Highers –

it was all done in the main hall – and we were all sitting there and I thought these questions are getting kind of difficult – you know, science and all this stuff - anyway afterwards I found out I should never have been there, I was only fourteen and the others who were sitting their Highers were seventeen. There were some who had been what we called 'kept back' and were in my class so I was doing advanced work, and so I made it – and people said 'You can't possibly have your Highers at fourteen. I said 'I do', and I had!

Pam Fairless started school at the Preparatory Department of Peebles High School:
It was run like a rural school with two teachers, one in charge of the Infant Room and the other in charge of the Upper Room and parents paid fees. In fact I had a friend visiting me, we had gone to school the same day, he and I, and he was laughing, saying he thinks it was 12s. 6d. a term[7]. I can't remember but it was something which today seems very paltry. There weren't many people went to this wee school, and I walked from Eliots Park to the High School every morning when I was five. Luckily there was a bus back at lunchtime and my mother always had the lunch on the table and then there was the bus back. But then we had to walk home at night from the High School but that was nothing in those days, because when the little school closed, I think when I was eight or nine, we went to Kingsland and some of the children there walked from Newby, you know, away up in the hills. They walked to Kingsland from there every day, never thought anything about it. I think we were much tougher in those days.[8] The school bell used to ring of course, Kingsland bell, to let the children know they had to start running when it was time for school to begin. I used to like the school bell ringing and then seeing the children running, and I was one of them.

But the thing I remember too was we played a lot in the playground. We were very organised, and even when I was at the preparatory at the High School, we always played at houses and we rushed out to get trees. We always had our houses at the foot of trees, and the one out first got the best tree. And the grass was sometimes allowed to grow really quite long so we flattened that down and made rooms. The Kingsland playground was the same, there was a lot of organised play there. Girls and boys were <u>kept completely separate.</u> There was a boys' playground down at the

---
[7] 62.5 pence.
[8] Mrs Minto, now aged 97, was the daughter of the shepherd at Upper Kidston. She told us she used to walk over Hamilton Hill every day to reach Kingsland School. She had to take a 'piece' which she ate in a shelter in the playground at lunchtime. Her father told her always to keep her back to the wind on Hamilton Hill.

bottom that had a football pitch and the girls were at the top part. We were mainly playing at houses and different games like that – High Tig or something – we always seemed to be very organised.

My mother thought it was good for me to go to Kingsland because she thought it would toughen me up because I had no brothers or sisters. And then I went to the High School and I went up in 1937 which was the first year of the new school – the extra bit that was added on at the top. I was at the first party to be held in the school hall – it was the first year party. I was quite happy at the school, but I don't think I was terribly academic. I liked sewing and I liked all the things that had nothing to do with using my brain very much. I was good at Maths but I wasn't an English student at all. I kept my friends, that's one of the things, like this friend who went to school on the same day and we have remained friends all our lives. We both had our golden weddings last year. I've kept in touch with quite a lot of my friends from that wee school that was up at the High School.

Peggy Ferguson and Mary Johnstone remember some of their teachers at Kingsland:
Peggy: Like Mary, I went to school at five at Halyrude. I thought it was eight we went up to Kingsland, or was it seven? I remember the awful feeling you could be kept back – do you remember that some could be kept back? Some were, if they were poor scholars. And I felt, oh, that was my one worry, in case I would be kept back. I thought that would be a terrible blow to be kept back, I wasn't, though. Do you remember Miss Forby, the first class teacher, Miss Forby?
Mary: No I didn't have her. Every year we moved on and every year we had one teacher.
Peggy: Well, we had Miss Forby in the first class.
Mary: I had Miss Johnston.
Peggy: And we had a wee woman, Miss Geralds was it? She played the piano for us all marching in. My sister had different teachers, she had Miss Logie.
Mary: I mind Miss Logie and Miss Barton.
Peggy: We had Miss Barton. Were you frightened of her?
Mary: The worst thing she did was to put the strap on the back of your head.
Peggy: She was always roaring. Miss Logie had a very hearty voice but Miss Barton was always roaring. If you were having trouble in the hall, which was at the centre of the school, you heard Miss Barton roaring all the time. She never did anything but tell you what to do.
Mary: 'Take your gym tunic off,' she roared, 'and get up these ropes.'

Sheila Laurie remembers teachers and friends of her school days:
I attended Halyrude School first where my teachers were Miss Bonong (a lovely lady) and Miss Shiel, another lovely lady. Then up to Kingsland School until qualifying for the High School at eleven. While attending Kingsland School, my friend Ella, who had an aunt and uncle farming at Upper Kidston, we would set off in the morning and walk over Hamilton Hill to Upper Kidston where we would play around, get milk and scones, collect the eggs and bring them back home. We also walked some Saturdays to Hundleshope Farm where Ella's other uncle and aunt farmed. The same procedure – only this walk was all on the roads, whereas Upper Kidston was hills and heather all the way. This would of course be summertime. I don't ever recall being tired. I suppose we chattered too much.

At school I played hockey and loved it. One of the teachers who took us for hockey was 'Fusht' Mackay. He was a great guy but was very excitable and was the butt of the older pupils. Funnily enough, he had been Dux when my mother was a junior student.

Arthur Crittell reflects how schools changed in Peebles and on his own school experiences:
When I was at school, there was Kingsland Primary School and St. Joseph's which was run by nuns, a lot of it, and the High School. St Joseph's school was where the garages are now, where the houses are, that was all the school – it's all Catholic ground now. The main part was where the hall is now, that was part of the school, and there were huts in the grounds that were part of the school and it was all enclosed by a green fence and there was a big field. That was in 1979, early 1980, they sold the ground off because they built Priorsford School and the Catholic School moved to Halyrude and there was a big controversy in the town about it at the time because a lot of people wanted the schools integrated, and people wanted the Catholics to integrate but the Diocese of the Catholic church wanted a separate school. A lot of people thought they should integrate the two schools because they integrated the High School.

I went to school at Halyrude for my first two years and my teachers there were Miss Clare and Miss Jack. Then there were two intakes at the school, one in the summer and one at Christmas and I went at the Christmas intake and Miss Clare was the first teacher – I was only five years old – and Miss Jack was the second teacher. And Miss Hearn – my father had Miss Hearn in the first year of infant school, and I had Miss Hearn in my last year at infant school.

Then I went to Kingsland School. Miss Sutherland was my first teacher at Kingsland and after lunch if you were very good and went straight to class, you might get a sweetie from her, great big pineapple chunks that you could hardly get in your mouth. And Miss Tweeddale and Miss Harper and Mr O'Hara. The headmaster was a man called Charlie Blackwell, who was very, very good, very much ahead of his time. He served in the Navy in the Second World War, very much a disciplinarian, very good teacher, very good headmaster. He introduced school educational cruises – a big thing then. I went when I was twelve to Denmark, Poland and Norway – we were supposed to go to Norway but we got fog-bound in the Baltic so we went to Sweden. When we were in Poland, we met people who had been in Peebles during the war.[9]

Jean Thomson remembers some of her High School teachers:
After my twelfth birthday, in 1945, I went up to the High School, and we were in what at that time was the new part, but now is about the second oldest, I think it would be. There was the old stone-built building, we went there for science and music and commercial. And in the new building, there was a long corridor downstairs and then you came upstairs. That's where we had our English and geography and history and maths. And we had nicknames for all our teachers – I can say that as most of them are away. There was Mrs McFarlane and we called her Fiery; she was our maths teacher, she was a good teacher but she was fiery. And our English teacher was a Miss Turnbull. We called her the Freak, but she made me take an interest in Shakespeare because, it must have been at the end of the first year in her English class, and the following year we were going to be starting reading some Shakespeare plays, and she said, 'At the end of term we'll do a Shakespeare play, "A Midsummer Night's Dream"' and we were more or less acting it out. She was really funny at it and she made me have a love for Shakespeare.

There used to be rural schools in small communities round Peebles. Pam Fairless recalled her eight and a half years from 1963 in Stobo when her husband was head teacher of the school there which had about 19 pupils spread between Primary 1 and Primary 7. It was 'like a little family'. [10]
Kinnaird Cunningham describes a similar school in Manor Valley:
Schools – well, they've changed, because we don't have a school in Manor Valley any longer. We had a very nice little school with one teacher – that's all we could justify for eighteen to twenty kids. I always thought they got quite a good education, but sometimes when they went to second school they found that they were not as bright as they thought they were, because they were brighter than the other locals who were at the primary school but not up to the standard of Peebles. And the school eventually closed in '76, '77, somewhere about then, and it will never open again.

---
[9] See Chapter 7 for Poles in Peebles during the war.
[10] Mr Fairless's time at Stobo School is described in Tales of Old Villagers' by Brian Martin.

Bessie Johnstone, looking back over her childhood and school days, describes a full and energetic life, with lots of happiness but with some solemn moments too:

Looking back, we had a wonderful childhood. We had the ruined Cross Kirk to play in because it was at the bottom of our garden. Looking back we seemed to be out and about, we were never still, we didn't know what 'bored' meant. We used to go on picnics – it wasn't lemonade then, it used to be Boston cream. I think it was made with lemons and I remember you made it with baking soda and tartaric acid and when you mixed it in, it foamed. We always had it in old lemonade bottles and you took it with you. We used to go right up the top of Venlaw and come out behind the Hydro.

At night, they had March Street Rovers and Rosetta Road Rangers – that was all the children from the streets – and they used to meet at Kirkland Street, the Post Office used to be there and that's where we played at night. There were no standing games, we always seemed to be running or pushing each other or something – 'Run, sheep, run' and 'Stockie-in' – and when you got older – it was terrible – you'd go into the closes and tie the two houses with ropes and rang the door for the people. We all got out to play at night. We had our curfew – in the summertime it was as long as the daylight, if you didn't have school the next day. You had to do your school work before you got out. You usually tried to do it before your teatime – you were desperate to get out. Of course we had tennis, we had the hard courts, across where the courts are now but further down. And we used to climb the walls to get into Hay Lodge Park because it was private ground then – the Thorburns were in Hay Lodge House. We called the walls up there the Cammel Dykes, that long wall from the hospital up to Neidpath. We climbed in there to get to the Cushie-doo, a big tree with a tree house where the pigeons roosted. We weren't allowed in there but funnily enough we never got chased out. Nobody did damage – there wasn't vandalism like there is now. We weren't all angels. I remember one fight – one of the boys who stayed underneath us was a nasty, nasty boy, he was always hitting somebody smaller, and one time his mother came up and had a dose of argument with me because I hit him with a marble - I had a marble in my hand – and I had hit him on the head with it – but he frightened all the kids round about.

When we came up to Rosetta Road – I must have been five when we came up here – one of my friends stayed round.in Graham Street and two stayed down in March Street – the four of us were together all the time. You went up to the big school at seven from Halyrude and you qualified at twelve, and if you passed the qualifier you went to the High School, and if you didn't you stayed and could become queen.[11]   The teachers used to take us for walks in the country and one time it must have been down at Horsburgh Castle and we came home sitting on the huge tree trunks on the horse-drawn cart piled high with felled trees.   And we used to walk up to Neidpath and come home on the turnip cart.

My school days were very happy – oh, there were the usual grumbles! I read an awful lot – I still do.   And during the winter we were continually in and out each other's houses.   We played dominoes and cards and all sorts of things and you had a stamp album and albums where you put your scraps – you stuck them in – and you used to barter scraps with each other – 'I'll give you two for that one…I'll give you two wee ones for your big one.'   I had a scrap book with all foreign scraps in – scraps of Japanese ladies and things like that.   You got them on sheets and you broke them up and stuck them in.   I think we probably did scraps on nights when we were glad to sit down when we came in.

I was lucky because an awful lot of other fathers didn't come home (from the First World War) but dad did, and dad played a lot with us.   He played 'Run, sheep, run' and he taught us a lot of card games, pelmanism and all these sorts of things. Did you play pelmanism? Well, we played that.   There was an old pack of cards and they all got turned up at the edges.   And he was a good drawer – he used to draw things for us.   He would draw something and then ask us what it was.   I think I was favoured because I was in the middle.   My mother was quiet but sometimes my dad used to flare up.

I can remember the day my grandmother died.   My younger brother was only three and I must have been eight and we were given money to go to the pictures on a Saturday afternoon.   Now we were never allowed to go to the pictures in the summertime, never.   When I came back everything was very quiet and my grandmother had died.   She was at home, we all stayed together, and she had been ill, and they must have known it was near the end, and we were put out of the house, of course, and when we came back in everything was quiet and my mother had been crying.   And my dad said to me, 'Gran has died,' and I said, 'Where is she?' and he said, 'In the bedroom.'   Well, I shared the bedroom with my grandmother, I had a truckle bed under her bed, and I did not want to go into the room, and dad said, 'Now she never hurt you in her life, she'll not hurt you now,' and he took my hand and took me in.   And he'd always given her his first sweet peas from the garden and when I went through, she had a bunch of fresh-sweet peas and I've never been afraid of death since.   That was a sensible sort of thing to do, wasn't it, looking back?   I have no recollection of how she looked but I remember her hand with the sweet peas in them.

---

[11] See Chapter 5 for Beltane Queen.

Bessie found this recipe for Boston Cream in a cookbook of 1930:
1 oz. Tartaric Acid   2 teaspoonfuls Essence of Lemon
1 breakfastcup of Sugar   1 white of Egg
2 and a half breakfastcups of Boiling Water
Pour boiling water over sugar, stirring occasionally.   When cold, add acid and essence and well-whipped white of egg. Bottle, take two tablespoonfuls to one tumbler of water and half a saltspoonful carbonate of soda.

David Tait and Jimmy French shared the same great-grandfather and were brought up like brothers.   Together, they sometimes got up to dangerous games, as their story tells:
I remember that the quarry up at the back of Venlaw was used as a firing range and when we were about eight to ten years old we went up there and there were these ammunition stores.   Some older lads had kicked the doors in and they had been in and left them open. We went in and there were grenades in boxes.   So boys being boys, we took a box of these grenades and we took them off up the hill to a place that we called Hunters Rock, and we tried to find how they worked.   I found the instructions on the lid.   It said they needed to be primed. We found the primer and unscrewed the base plate, put the primer in, screwed the base plate back on and there it was, ready.   So we took one back to the quarry and threw it over the top and it went off. The branches and all sorts of stuff went flying in the air.   And do you know what we did?   We went into the police station and told them that there was somebody playing with grenades up in the quarry, and they went flying up there and we got recommended for being good boys for reporting the theft.   We could easily have killed someone or even ourselves.   There was only a four second delay on the fuse and you can't get far in four seconds!

Duncan Taylor has stories to tell too:
We used to go out into the countryside and every time – boy or girl – we'd have a catapult.   I mean, I was a crack shot with a catapult!
   I'll tell you another story.   Stuart – his father was an admiral in the Navy. We all had tacket boots and in the winter we all used to slide on them, on the pavements.   But Stuart had shoes with leather soles and he couldn't slide on them.   No tacketty boots!   His father was awfully good to him and gave him all the fancy toys, but I'll never forget that – he was always greeting[12] because he couldn't have tacketty boots!   He wanted to be the same as everyone else.   Aye, we had great fun with the big slides, and he wasn't getting any.

---
[12] i.e. complaining

Willie Euman also remembered the pursuits of boyhood:
What did we do, you asked me what did we do? Everything, the answer's everything. Climbing trees, going up Soonhope Glen, jumping the burn – there wasn't a bit of Soonhope burn we hadn't leapt. Some were considerable leaps. It took the best of the company, usually my brother Sandy and a guy called Alan Matthieson who would manage the extra difficult leaps.

What did we do? Nesting – and I never remember taking many eggs although we did take one, but mother, to whom we perhaps enjoy our considerable interest in the great outdoors, she always said, 'Well, if you must take an egg, just take one and be careful not to damage.' I should stress that this was an earlier day and age when it wasn't a crime to collect eggs. Everybody had a collection at that age and it never seemed to diminish bird stocks.

When chestnut time came, we were always out after chestnuts. There was always a particular challenge who would get the biggest chestnut. We didn't wait for them to fall off the trees, we would hurl sticks up into the treetops and bring down a deluge of chestnuts. Sometimes some of our number were unfortunate to get the stick down on their heads too!

And then, at Eshiels, two miles east of Peebles, there was MacGillivary's nursery and we were always eager to get our names on their list for the strawberry picking. So perhaps three or four weeks down there picking strawberries, during the early period of the summer, the school summer holidays.

Isabel Taylor's memories of strawberry picking were a little different!
When we were young, we swam in the river, that's where we spent our summer holidays as children. We were thrown out in the morning by our parents and just played in the river and fished – it was a wonderful place to play. In the school holidays, there was no option, we were told to take sisters and brothers – 'You want to take your sister along? .....You will take your sister!' And all big brothers, didn't they, Duncan, had their sisters to look after. We used to go along the old railway up there – there used to be a farm out there, MacGillivary's, and we used to go and get strawberries in summer. All the children went up the railway to get these strawberries. They used to get a gun and they used to fire at us, not to hit us, over our heads. That used to make us run but we still got quite a few strawberries into the bargain, didn't we, Duncan?

And Peggy and Mary described the mischief that they got up to:
Mary: Well, we played Tig and Stockie.
Peggy: We never played that at school, we played that at nights. It was just like Hide and Seek, but when you ran back to the den, you would shout,

'Stockie-In'.   Stockie and Hide and Seek – there was a great tree and there was always somebody hiding behind it – the first place you looked if you were running for the den.

Mary: We were never off Venlaw Hill when we were all young. We were always away up there.

Peggy: And in the lower parts, there were a lot of raspberries there. We used to go to a place way down at Scotsmill. Before you come to Scotsmill, we turned right, you crossed a wee stream, we used to climb the gate and go away up, slanting we used to call it, the field and with another hill to climb and oh, the raspberries! It was at the back of the White Brig. Well we went there and picked raspberries, and you know before we got home, the juice was really beginning to come through the bags, bursting you know, and we got covered. We just got in the door and my mother would get the pan out and the jam was made in no time.

Mary: Oh aye. And then we used to pinch apples. At Hay Lodge was best. They had an orchard at Hay Lodge big house, it's still there, and they had loads of apple trees. And the boys used to say, 'Right, you're watching. You need to see if the police are coming.'

Peggy: And if the police caught you, you'd get a wallop across the ear! And, 'I'll tell your mother!' But even so, you respected the police in those days, and you would go to them if you had something wrong.

Mary: But when we were young, we never did anything serious. You know the bells they had in the old times? We used to pull all the bells and run, that was our biggest crime, that and pinch apples at Hay Lodge.

Fig. 5   Peebles High Street as our contributors' parents and grandparents knew it.

Chapter 3

MARKETS, FARMING AND FORESTRY

Until very recently, the people of Peebles were much more closely in touch with the farming community that lived and worked around them. The weekly cattle market was part of the rhythm of town life reflected in the childhood memories we have collected.

From Ian Brunton:
In the 1930's, the annual sheep sales were held in a sheep ring, which was located in Clark Place, at the North end of Cross Street where there are now Council houses. At the time of the major lamb sale in September and October, on Fridays, all the streets of Peebles were filled with never ending flocks of sheep, separated only by dogs and red-faced shepherds. Needless to say, sheep strayed into gardens and the fun for the town's youngsters increased when housewives brandishing brooms etc joined in the fray. Many of the flocks in town on those Fridays had been on the road for three or four days, coming as they did from West Linton, Tweedsmuir and Broughton. There were no sheep lorries in those days.

And Sheila Murray:
Before the Auction Mart of farm animals was moved to South Park a few years after the war, it was situated in Montgomery Place where the Clark Place houses now stand. Sheep were transported by train to the station in the Caledonian Road and driven by shepherds and their collies over Tweed Bridge, up Elcho Street Brae (not one way at that time) and along Cross Street to the sale ring, which was a hive of activity every Friday and a place of excitement and interest for us children. The town was always extra busy on market day. The present Edinburgh Woollen Mill was a tearoom in those days called 'The Pillars' and was popular with the country folk on sale days. Across the road was Wilson and Sime's bakery with a very nice restaurant upstairs – very popular with locals as well as visitors. Here the farming community could have a substantial high tea before heading for home. Farm collies could be seen waiting patiently outside the Neidpath Inn in the Old Town while their masters slaked their thirst inside. The

auctioneer had a farm outside the town and on market day came into Peebles in a pony and trap. After a visit to the Neidpath Inn, the auctioneer, having imbibed too freely, frequently had to be helped into the trap and the pony found its own way home.

One of Jean Thomson's earliest memories is of a rather alarming visit to the market:
My cousins came to stay in the September of 1937, when I was four years old, and I can remember the one called Mary took me round to the cattle market one day in Clark Place, and they had all the pens set up, the wooden pens, for the sheep. There must have been cattle and I don't know what else, and I remember there was quite a panic. I remember a man came and put the two of us in beside some sheep, so whether an animal had got loose, I'm not really sure – it could have been a bull or anything – and I can remember us being pushed in beside sheep which would be more safe.

Pam Fairless had alarming meetings with animals in the street, and remembers happy visits to the farm up the road from her house:
When I was young, the town was much smaller. The sale ring for the cattle and the sheep was where Clark Place is, in the centre of the town, and on a Friday it was sale day, and when I was walking away up to the High School, I didn't like it very much if I met cattle on the road as they were herded along. All the sheep and cattle were brought over the drove roads right to the centre of Peebles, and the streets were a bit of a mess as well! I was always scared when I met cows being herded through, and there was always a collie dog or two as well. And the sheep just swarmed right across the road and you had to stand in a doorway until they passed.

As children we found the Watson's farm – Eliots Park Farm – a great attraction. Mr and Mrs Watson lived there with their son Alex. The road up to the farm led between the Rosetta Estate boundary, a dry-stone dyke, on one side and the back gardens of Eliots Park, and then a field on the other. In summer, this field was full of buttercups and it was here that the cows grazed. A burn ran through the field, under the road and into a wood on the other side. We played games jumping from stone to stone and with 'soldiers' (as we called the plantains) which grew at the roadside. I can remember horse tails, broom and lots of marguerites growing there too.

The farmhouse sat low at the top of the incline and cobbles led to the scrubbed doorstep covered in a curly pattern made by Mrs Watson with a whitening stone. The house had no running water and was served by a spring beside the byre at the edge of the golf course. All water had to be fetched and carried from the spring, where the water-beetles paddled, but where the water was pure and clear. We children were sent with a basket for the weekly eggs or a pitcher to buy milk. I can remember yet the chill air of the small dairy, where Mrs Watson dipped the little measure with the long hooked handle into the huge can with the big lid, and filled my pitcher with milk. Mrs Watson would sometimes be baking scones on a griddle over the range fire when we called and we were sure to be given a bit spread with butter and occasionally a glass of milk. In summer we sat on the seat outside the door in front of the kitchen window to eat it, but in winter we occupied the little window seat in the cosy low-ceilinged kitchen with its range and dresser.

The arrival of a new calf was an excitement and we were taken to see it. Once, aged five, dressed in my new school blazer, I stood in the byre admiring the new calf and let the cow lick my blazer all over – returning home in a bit of a mess! The Watson's kept a great number of hens and I imagine that is how they made most of their living. Alex entered the enclosures and the hens all rushed towards him as he scattered the grain with a sweep of his hand and arm. I loved to watch, but I loved best of all when we were allowed to go to see the newly-hatched chicks in the big hut round the back. The hut was cosy inside, heated by an incubator in the centre of a large waist-high table, edged with mesh netting, and there we saw the fluffy chicks, some brown and some yellow, constantly moving and cheeping. We got to hold one in our hands which was a great thrill.

Bessie Johnstone took an active part in market days, and knew the local farming families:
On market days, we used to help the farmers take their sheep home. When we moved up to Rosetta Road, the market was behind us at the bottom of the garden, and we used to go in there and help the men put the sheep into the pens and then we'd help take them up the road back to their farms. There were no lorries, the men had to walk the sheep up. We'd walk them up to Edston, and sometimes we'd walk them up to Neidpath Castle to keep them from straying – that was wonderful. We knew the Cairns from Edston – they came to school – and the girls from Neidpath who came to school – they all had to walk. And we knew the Jacks up at Edderston Farm of course, at the top of Edderston Road.

Margaret Jack tells of family life and work at Edderston Farm:
My family has been in Peebles for over a hundred years so we've been here for quite a wee while. My grandfather sold milk and his name was George

Jack and he was called Jinglin' Geordie because of the coins jingling in his money bag, and we have a very old photograph of him in the High Street with his milk cart.[1] The family had a dairy at the foot of the Old Town to begin with and then it moved about half way up the Old Town and that was Jack's Dairy, opposite the Cassoway house. We had a farm up South Parks and in fact that's where the saleroom used to be but this was before the saleroom was there, and I was actually born in the house that's been converted into flats now. And from there we moved up to Edderston Farm where my great uncle and aunt were, and I think they had been there for about a hundred years as well, and that's where we lived most of our lives, but now we've given up farming and live in the town.

I think we maybe had about 40 to 60 milking cows – it was quite big. At first we milked by hand and then we got the machines. And we had to go each day from there to take the milk to the Dairy in the town. I was the youngest in the family and I had four brothers. I had to clean their shoes but as far as the farm work was concerned, I think they made it easy for me. I was always a wee bit nervous of the animals, I was always a wee bit wary of them.

We used to go to the smithy, which was at Whitebridge down the road. That was where the smith worked, a man called Johnny Bruce, but we had our jobs done at the smithy at Edderston and my uncle used to go down in the car to bring them up to shoe the horses, and they had a bellows and a fire and the horseshoes. We had maybe three or four Clydesdales in my day. I can tell you a story about that – my aunt, who was a nursing sister, was in the Middle East during the war, nursing, and she was in the officers' mess and there was a copy of The Scotsman lying on the table and she picked up this newspaper to have a look at it and there was a photograph in it of Back Sware with my brother and Willie Gilchrist who worked on the farm ploughing on Back Sware, a field near Manor Sware bridge. There were two horses at the plough. Now imagine that! That picture was in The Scotsman!

Two brothers took over the farm from our parents, but they were only half time for a while and they decided the work was so hard, they gave up the farming and got jobs in the town. They hadn't been off at Christmas or New Year for forty years! They had two really bad harvests, the weather was really bad, and they just decided to get out. We missed the farm, we were all heart-broken, but we had an easier life. The farm's still going strong; it actually didn't belong to us, it belongs to the Earl of Wemyss, it's his land, so we were just tenant farmers; he has never sold it and the land is still his.

---

[1] See Chapter 8 for the photograph of the milk cart.

Fig. 6 Harrowing with Clydesdale horses on Edderston Farm,
looking towards Neidpath Castle across Tweed.

Colonel Sprot of Crookston looks back over decades of change in the valleys south of Peebles, and the unchanging nature of hill farming:

My grandmother, my mother's mother and mother of my uncle at Haystoun, used to spend every summer of her widowed life up at Glensax, the old shepherd's house right at the head of the Glen, three miles up from Haystoun. We children used to spend two or three weeks of our holidays there. We always went up by pony and trap – absolutely wonderful – and we used to put night lines out in the burn and have fresh fish for breakfast.

By the early sixties, my uncle, who was well over eighty, had kindly made me his heir because he didn't have any children.[2] When I came back in 1962, I went and looked after Haystoun for him but he died fairly soon after and I became luckily the owner so I was very busy farming three farms and looking after the forests and so on. I had a payroll of six. There wasn't just the farm, it was also the gamekeeping side and the forestry side.

The four farms in this area, Hundleshope, Crookston, Bonnington and Haystoun Home Farm[3], they were all really stock farms. Bonnington Farm was a let farm, next door to Haystoun and it was originally a dairy farm and it had just changed to stock, mostly cattle, and the tenant there, shortly after I got back, in the sixties, had a great celebration because their family had been tenants of my family for a hundred years, which was rather nice, and there was a great close relationship between the two families. These were all really stock farms and all except Bonnington had a hill – of varying sizes. Quite a biggish one on Hundleshope, very small one here at Crookston, and the Home Farm which is Newby and Glensax, a very large hill – large in acreage but very small in carrying capacity. Low ground, to make quite a good comparison, low ground they say four ewes to an acre, on the hill it's four acres to the ewe. That's sixteen times bigger carrying capacity down below than it is on the hill. On the hills, we raise Blackface, although South Country Cheviots is another hill breed, but virtually it's Blackface on a black hill and a black hill means a heather hill, and Cheviots are on a white hill, which is a grass hill, hence the expression black and white hills. And down below on the low ground, really whatever sheep one wanted and I think mostly Border Leicester was the great tup sheep – the male was a Border Leicester – and Greyface which is a cross with the Blackface – they were the original basic sheep that all the crosses came from. And with cattle, the Highland and the Galloway were the very original and all the others were the exotics that have now come in.

---

[2] This was Sir Duncan Hay. The Hays of Yester had land in this valley, called Common Struther, from at least as far back as the late fifteenth century, as well as serving down the centuries in different official capacities in the Burgh of Peebles, as is shown in documents printed in Charters and Documents of the Burgh of Peebles, 1165-1710, Scottish Burghs Records Society, 1872.

[3] See account of John Brown on p.43.

Over the years, so much has changed, but because everything is so gradual, you don't notice the change at the time. I suppose mechanisation is the biggest change – I mean there are no ponies and no traps now – but it's all gradually happened. Even in a house, there was always electricity of a sort. Many people had their own little generator and then one had an open range in the kitchen before the days of Esses and Agas[4] and before the days of electric cookers. When I got back in the sixties, I found that the farm cottages on the whole place had been modernised post war, but my goodness that modernity was not what one had in the sixties and seventies so they all had to be done again. The three cottages each got an extra bedroom. The bathroom and the kitchen used to be all in one so we cut off a bit of the top bedroom and made new bathrooms and put a WC down below to use when they came in off the farm for their dinner. They're all now at the time to be redone. So that probably is one of the biggest changes. I don't think the land itself has changed except they're getting more new types of fertilisers, and machinery – all these wonderful big enormous tractors you see working. They go out feeding the stock and there are all these big round bales which can only be carried on the front of a tractor. In my day we only had all those small bales and you could carry two yourself with the strings. Now they have quad bikes for herding sheep but my shepherd up Glensax much preferred his pony. The advantages of a pony that he and I both realised were that you are that much higher and to be able to see over high ground. It had to be a well trained pony so you could get off and leave it while you dealt with a sick ewe and you could carry things over the saddle. A horse, you relied on it, it knew where it was going and wouldn't fall down a precipice.

A hill farm is really, you might say, run by nature – the weather and everything. Some people try to make the hill ewes lamb a little bit earlier but we always lambed here, these high bits, mid-April to mid-May, and one would be quite happy to be even later because there was no grass to eat. This high bit here, the grass never grew till the end of April and the ewes didn't have much milk. That's not changed for hill places but there's so much artificial feeding, artificial fertiliser, to bring on the grass in the lowground bits so that has changed. It's so nice that the hills really can't change much. .

There used to be the market at Clark Place – that's up the back of March Street – then it moved to the bottom of Edderston Road, at the dead end – that was the market until about ten years ago. I sold all my cattle there, and my sheep. Everything's changed so much now, very few markets –

---

[4] Esses and Agas were solid-fuel-burning cookers.

it's all done either on the computer or they go straight to the slaughterhouse. The market drew people to Peebles and was a wonderful social occasion. One always drove home very worried one wasn't going to get home. We all went in and had dram after dram. There were some maddening things. I got rather fed up with the awful luckpenny. Anyone who bought things from you almost always demanded a luckpenny. You would be rudely accosted by the buyer, 'I bought those heifers of yours. I want a luckpenny.' Sometimes you got away with a tenner. I was far too embarrassed when I bought my blackie tups ever to ask for a luckpenny!

Kinnaird Cunningham remembers how farming used to be in Manor Valley:
Everybody used to grow barley and everybody had a reaper-binder for cutting it, and mostly still with horses when we arrived but tractors came in very soon after. We would all go down and stook it, eight sheaves to a stook, and we would spend days doing that, and then when they were all dry, it had to be put into stacks, and that again was quite an interesting exercise as the stack got higher and higher and if you were on top laying out the sheaves, you wondered how you were ever going to get down – we just slid down as far as I remember – but it was a big employer of labour and we all used to have to go to help with the harvest. People helped one another quite a lot. They were quite heavy when they were wet, those stooks, and after a day of putting the sheaves into stooks, you did not want to do much else, or forking with the hayfork up on to the stack when it was getting higher, it was a day's quite hard work when you were young. The old experts made it look very easy, us young people used to make a lot of effort and use a lot of muscles we didn't know we had, and we suffered. Elevators came in much later, up here anyway, and I can't remember when the first combine appeared up here, but it was well into the seventies.

A mobile threshing machine used to come along, grinding along the road. You used a hayfork getting sheaves off the stack into the threshing machine, with all the dogs rushing around trying to catch the rats that come out. The dust and straw and everything made you very dry and there used to be a plentiful supply of some sort of liquid depending on your age to keep you going.

Now there is no cultivated land except for one field of turnips in the whole Valley. Instead of growing turnips and seeing those poor Irishmen in the middle of winter singling the turnips, now it's just all silage and grass. No dairy farm – a lot of beef cattle but we used to have a lot more dairy cattle. There are probably more horses now than there were then, because there were only working horses then and very few riding ones, and now the place is littered with riding horses and no working horses of course at all. Sheep – they used to be mostly Blackface, and now they're all sorts and they're kept in in the winter or kept down on the low ground whereas in the old days they used to be up on the hills. The poor old shepherd had to go and find them when the weather was bad – on his feet, not on a quad bike.

Farmworkers would be expected to dyke when there wasn't any other work to be done. I don't think there were many full time dykers. Mostly the farm lads did it themselves, because there were times when they weren't that busy on the farm. They certainly built some remarkable drystone dykes earlier on, but in the fifties, sixties, seventies they were just trying to repair them, put them back up again as they'd fallen down, rather than building brand new dykes. A dyke will last a hundred years or more, no bother, if it's well built. Even dykes I built forty, fifty years ago are still standing.

There used to be four mills in Manor Valley but they all gradually went out because it wasn't worth keeping them going for a small amount of barley or oats.

John Brown ponders on generations of farming in his family and reflects how farming methods and the farming community have changed since the 1950s. But has it been progress?

My family came to the Haystoun Estate in 1868 from Biggar – that was my mother's family, they were Russell, and they farmed Haystoun until about 1890 and then my grandfather got the tenancy of Bonnington Farm and that's where I was born and brought up. Bonnington and Haystoun were part of the Haystoun estate – it was Sir Duncan Hay at that time – that's Colonel Sprot's uncle – and then the Colonel came in 1962 – he retired from the army in '62 and he was the landlord after that and he isn't now because he's handed it over to his niece – Mrs Coltman – but the Colonel is a real gentleman – a fine man the Colonel. He's been a big asset to the Shire you know – he was Lord Lieutenant until he retired from the post.[5] My nephew still farms at Bonnington and I farmed at Hundleshope which is another farm on the estate in Manor parish. My father came here when my grandfather died in 1938. His father farmed at Burn Foot at Eddleston

The Browns started at Bonnington then – it was Russell before that. My brother was born at Windylaws and by the time I was born in 1939 they were at Bonnington. So I was a pre-war baby, only just and it was during the war that things really changed in agriculture.

---

[5] See p.86 for Colonel Sprot's account of his time as Lord Lieutenant.

My grandfather had been a very progressive man and he had introduced tractors and milking machines and my father carried on, and of course the emphasis during the war was to produce as much food as they could. There was a lot of land ploughed up and put into grain because of war time measures, and I remember – I must have been about five or six - the big travelling thrashing mill came twice a year – this was a kind of highlight – and it would work for maybe four days or five days thrashing quite a lot of grain. At that time we had to get help – there was the Land Army at that time – the women in the Land Army used to come out and help with the thrashing – that's some of my earliest memories.

Of course we had no electricity at that time, it was paraffin lamps and there was actually a thrashing machine in the steading, in the barn, and it was driven by a water wheel and the water wheel also drove the suction pump that worked the milking machines. There was a pond up the valley a wee bit - a burn fed the pond – and I remember in the bad winter of 1947 my father had to go up every morning and clear the grating that took the water from the burn into the pond as it got crusted up and filled up with snow. It was so deep at one time he had a five or six foot ladder to get down into the burn so that he could clear out that grating in the morning to get the water into the pond so that the mill wheel would work to milk the cows – a twice a day operation.

Fig. 7   Thrashing machine at Bonnington Farm, 1920s.   John's Grandmother Russell is holding the milk pail.

We got the electricity put in in 1948 in Bonnington – one of the earliest farms in the county, I would say, because it was the fifties before some of them got electricity. That transformed things as far as farming life was concerned – you went and just pressed a button to do things with electric motors and put down a switch instead of working with lanterns and lamps – that was one of my early memories of the farm.

At that time there was very little fertiliser used, just manure from the cows and the sheep. After the war the first bagged fertiliser was used and at that time it was spread by hand. When we were boys we used to carry pails from the bags to my father and some of the men and they had sheets in front of them, just as if they were sowing grain and that's how you spread the fertiliser. And the stocking density on the ground now – you have about 5 sheep to the acre – and at that time when there was no fertiliser there were one and a half ewes to the acre and that's how production has increased over the years. At that time the grain was cut with a binder. I can only remember one horse being on the farm. There was one horse and it did odd jobs. Everything was done with tractors – they had no tyres, of course, just metal wheels with big steel lugs in them. For harvesting it was a binder. It dropped the sheaves out the back and they were put on a cart and put into stacks and then the stacks were thatched and it was a very time consuming operation. My father by this time had Haystoun Farm as well – he got Haystoun back again in 1949 – there were 10 men working on the two farms, including my brother and me, and now there's one man in each farm.

Fig. 8   Reaper-binder at work at Bonnington Farm, 1930s.

By 1950 my father bought his own thrashing mill – the chaps that were going around the farms had stopped and he bought his own and a big baler that went behind it and I remember saying at the time, 'Well that'll see me now, that'll do me all my life' and in ten years it was out of date, it was completely obsolete, the combines came in and we got our first combine about 1956, 1957. It worked with bags, the grain was bagged up and then you had to cart the bags, and it wasn't long before we had the tanker combines. The grain went in a big tank and it discharged into a trailer and all these things cut the need for labour down.   You could do in a day what it took all these men almost a week to do – there was that much difference. At that time of course we had a market in Peebles - an auction market – and we naturally resold all our livestock in Peebles market – it was very handy – you could actually chase the sheep down there, you didn't need to cart them.   Ours were not that far out and we could take a couple of hundred down at a time and just make sure somebody had to go and shut all the garden gates to make sure they didn't go in anybody's garden and we just chased them down to the market – you couldn't do it now there's so much traffic on the road, but at that time there wasn't the traffic. We had a car but that was the only car on the farm.   My father had a car but none of the chaps that worked for him had a car.   There was a bus, a good bus service, used to go down Manor Valley and come down twice or thrice a week and their wives could get the bus to get to Peebles but there's not been country buses now for thirty years.   We've lost our local market now and our livestock gets carted to Stirling now – it's a long way. The nearest working markets are 35 miles away, either St. Boswells or Lanark or Stirling – it involves more transport. And there's less slaughterhouses – a lot of the lambs now are being carted all over England and Wales to be slaughtered – it's a sign of the times.

In the middle fifties, that was the most prosperous time that was in farming, I would say, in my lifetime.   Take wages – the men were probably working for about £7 - £8 a week and father was getting about £5 for a lamb that was ready for the market so two lambs would pay a man for a week and now it would take ten lambs to pay a man for a week so wages have gone up and the price of food hasn't gone up comparatively – Harold MacMillan said we'd never had it so good and as far as agriculture was concerned we never had it so good and at that time there wasn't a lot of support from government.   In marginal areas there was some support but not a lot, nothing to what it has progressed under the Common Market and the European Community – now you couldn't farm in Peeblesshire without Community Support, at that time you could.

I went to College in 1955, agricultural college, and travelled by train to Edinburgh every day, with a nice wee diesel train that went from Peebles to

Edinburgh every day, took an hour, and I finished in 1960. My wife, Ann, was at teaching school, Moray House, and that's where we really met - we went to school together but we didn't have anything to do with one other until we met on the train again. So we got married in 1960 and we stayed at Bonnington then. And at that time we were earning £10 a week, that's what we got, and we were quite well off, actually, we thought we were quite well off at £10 a week. That shows how things have changed, too.

There was a shepherd at Bonnington when I was young, and when the last shepherd retired when my brother left school – he was three and a half years older than me and didn't want to go to college – he took over as shepherd and we never had a shepherd after that. When I came back from college, I milked the cows and my brother was the shepherd. At shearing time, we had six neighbours who came to us and my father would go to them. There would probably be a dozen – some staff on the farm and half a dozen chaps come from round about. The clipping was done by hand at that time and then the wool was all rolled up and packed into sheets before it went away. My brother and I clipped the sheep ourselves once mechanical clipping came in, then, when we decided we were too old, in the last twenty years there's been a squad comes in and they can clip hundreds in a day – it's so much quicker with the machines. But funnily enough the wool still goes away in exactly the same kind of sheets as it did then. We had to have big sheets that would hold about fifty fleeces and the wool's still bundled up in these big sheets and that's how they're sold and that hasn't changed at all. You hear of big balers in Australia, but that's never happened here. The sheep are clipped in a different way but the wool still handled exactly the same.

On Bonnington we had about four hundred ewes and there were a hundred cows in the dairy. That's quite a big dairy – we were one of the biggest dairies in the shire at that time. A couple of dairies in the town would come out and get the milk but I remember when I was just eight or nine my father used to cart the milk to the train every morning in ten gallon cans and then in the early fifties, there was a lorry came on the job – I think the train was less than satisfactory and a lorry went round the whole county and lifted a whole load of cans – it was still ten gallon cans that were lifted on the lorry, and it went to the creameries in Edinburgh, although there was always a couple of dairies in the town that would maybe get twenty gallons. Both of these dairies had cows of their own and they got enough from us - some days they'd get twenty gallons, some days they'd get thirty - just to make it up. We used the ten- gallon cans up to 1970 and then there was a bulk tank put in at that time. My grandfather had one of the first milking machines in the shire. When the Highland

Show was at Peebles in 1906, which was held at Victoria Park, and my grandfather got this milking machine twenty, thirty years before many

Fig. 9 Milking machine at Bonnington Farm, 1906 model. Similar machines, working on unchanged principle, were in use at the Farm up to the 1970s.

farms; folk from the Highland Show visited to see it working. A lot of people were still milking by hand in the wartime and after the wartime. But there was always a milking machine at Bonnington, driven by the water wheel and that was a great step forward, because you needed a lot of folks to milk. When they used to hire folks, one of the agreements was a man had to have a wife and the wife had to be prepared to milk cows and a woman would probably milk 10 cows at a time so if you have 50 cows or 40 cows, you'd need four other wives to milk the cows. That never happened at Bonnington even in my mother's time because there was always a milking machine. It was quite funny because my grandfather actually profited by it because he was able to go and buy cows at market cheaper because the teats had to be a certain size to milk by hand and he could milk by machine. In the 1970s once the bulk tank came in, there was a pipeline went all round the whole of the byre and into the bulk tank that was refrigerated. We stopped milking at Bonnington in about 1978 because we were a big dairy but not big enough. Now there are four dairies left in Peeblesshire and they must have as many cows as the 65 dairy farms in Peeblesshire at the end of the war; the four will be producing more milk than the 65 would be then. All the smallholdings down Eshiels, every one was a dairy farm with 15 cows, 10 cows. A man and his family could make a living from milking these cows, and now you need 200 cows to make a living. That's how the countryside's got depopulated, of course; folk have come to live in the houses but they travel to Edinburgh to work. It's just how the economics of the farming job have changed completely in quite a short space of time. It wouldn't have changed for about two hundred years from the enclosures. The time of change came in the middle of the last century; from 1930 to 1960, that's when there was huge change in agriculture, completely from horses and hand labour to the '60s mechanisation. In the good old days, it was a hard, hard graft, there was a lot of hard work and men lived in sub-standard houses. Bonnington wasn't so bad because it only about a mile from the town but further up Manor Water – 7 or 8 miles – and the only way they could get there would be to walk or maybe a bus once a week, in the thirties, but the war really transformed things. That was when the boost was put into agriculture. My mother and father actually courted for about eight years because they could not afford to get married. They got married in 1935 and they had no money at all but they just decided that they were going to get married. And then just when the war came, farming was needed.

My mother always had a men's supper every Christmas and all the men who worked and there were quite a few casual ones, the likes of the local blacksmith and all the chaps from the estate would be there – probably as many as thirty came at Christmas. At haymaking time my mother and some of her helpers would bring out tea to feed the ten or twelve men because usually we worked until sundown if the weather was good in the summertime for the hay or the harvest. When we made hay, it was cut with a reaper and then it had to be turned with the forks and then it was made into ricks and then it was put into big stacks – really big stacks. Only one or two men were able to build these stacks as it was quite a skilled job to keep them standing so they didn't fall down. Then in the middle fifties we started baling the hay instead of making it into stacks. There was always a good squad and it made it a far more social time; we were young and had good fun. Now it's one solitary man sitting on a tractor and only his wireless going, whereas at that time we were working together and there was chatter and banter all the time and it was far more enjoyable. You were never working on your own in those days, there were always two or three of you about. With all the mucking out of the sheds done by hand and put on trailers and taken out and dumped in the fields and spread by hand, you were always working with somebody and it was far more sociable than it is now.

We grew potatoes at Bonnington and we used to get school children out from the school and it used to take about three or four days – maybe there'd be twenty school children, in the late fifties. I left the school in '55, and I was in charge of that squad and they were only maybe three years younger than me! We had mechanical potato diggers, of course, and each one had what we called a stent and a stent was maybe ten yards and they had maybe five or six baskets and they had to lift this stent, and it was often quite amusing because some of them were far better at it than others and of course the machine was ready to come up the next row and they wouldn't have finished lifting theirs and I used to hear, 'I've not finished yet, mister' and it was quite funny. Then the potatoes were put on a cart and they were pitted at that time, they were put in a clamp on the farm. The potato clamp (we call it a pit) was made by covering the potatoes with wheat straw and then six inches of soil on top, to make an inverted V-shaped pit. The potatoes sat in these clamp stores and they were there maybe till January or February and then they were put in sacks and taken away – some were sold locally but mostly to potato merchants - that was how the potatoes were handled – it was quite interesting really, they were put in one ton boxes by machines.

So farming since the fifties has just got more intensive than it was – more fertilisers being used and sprays came on that we never had before, and instead of growing maybe 25 cwt of grain to the acre you could grow 40 cwt – two tons - and there were the combines, and if we grew turnips or swedes, there was a machine that sowed individual seeds and it cut out all the need to thin them out – and all these labour saving things just show how agriculture has moved on to how it is at the present day.

Aidan Sprot describes how forestry too has changed over the years, and described his priorities when making new plantings:
The forestry background is changing. One used to plant and then thin and send all your thinnings as pit props, but now there are no pits to prop up and they seem to clear fell. See that hill opposite, which was the Bonnington Farm hill ground till my grandfather planted it in 1895. The timber was compulsorily purchased in the war, in the mid-forties. It was nothing like mature but they were obviously short of timber and nearly 360 acres were

felled.   In the war, when all the foresters were called up, my uncle couldn't undertake replanting 360 acres himself, so he sold the land to the Forestry Commission and that standing crop is what was planted in, I think, late forties, early fifties, and they are doing a lot now on it.   They're clear felling so much, but I think that is what they do now.

I always reckoned in my own woods that you took first thinnings out at thirty years old, depending how they did, and then you could do another thinning depending on what type of tree.   Hardwood trees one only planted really for shelter, not for a crop.   I used to say to people that in this valley priority is planting trees for shelter.   Because we get this terrible wind in this valley – it's unbelievable because it gets very narrow here – priority is shelter, next priorities are for sport, shooting and for amenity, to have decent-looking trees, so one always puts some hardwoods round, and the last is timber production, except in the big blocks.   We have one big block, the Lady Blair Plantation.   Anyone from the Forestry Commission was horrified when I told them timber production was the least important but shelter was predominant, and in the old days they all planted hardwood because these things like Sitka Spruce and so on hadn't come over to this country then and the hardwoods were very good.   They were terribly slow growers and then they had nothing down below because the old beech trees and oak and ash had all the foliage at the top so they really didn't give much shelter to stock and so one had to be fairly careful.   I hated felling the lovely ones and one had to fell in batches and plant the thing that people are so rude about – the Sitka Spruce – because it was a quick grower and gave you shelter quickly.   So in the end I was planting, instead of Sitka, only larch and Scots Pine, which are fairly quick growers and I usually tried to put hardwood on the outside of any of these shelter belts the whole way up the valley.

Chapter 4

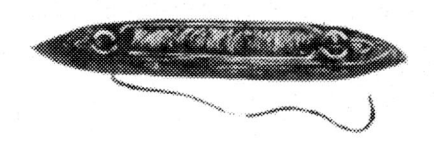

PEEBLES AT WORK

In Chapter 3, we heard about the farming community for which Peebles was the market centre. But for most people living in Peebles, their livelihood came not from the land but from industry and commerce. From the early nineteenth century until the 1960s, the mills were the dominant source of work in the town, and many of our contributors remembered the central place of the mills in the life of Peebleans.
Sheila Murray writes:
When I was a child in the 1930s, Peebles was a busy, bustling, thriving little town. The three mills provided jobs for close on a thousand workers. Two mills, Ballantynes and Thorburn, produced high quality tweed which was sold on the home markets and also exported to various countries abroad. They also wove tartans for the army. The third mill was Thorburn's spinning mill, situated where the baths stand now. This mill produced yarn for the manufacture of tweed. A familiar sound in the town was that of the mill horns, signalling starting time at 7.45 or 8 o'clock, midday dinner time and 5.30 finishing time, and tall mill chimneys dominated the skyline as well as sending out thick, black smoke. Lowe Donald's warehouse in the Station Road (now Holland and Sherry) stocked tweeds from the local mills and fine worsted from Yorkshire. The cloth was cut into lengths for suits and coats and sent worldwide.

Many families, like that of Pam Fairless, had generations of connection with the mills:
My father was a wool sorter in Thorburn's Tweedside Mills. My grandfather had been one as well, my Grandfather Robson. My granny had been a weaver at Walkerburn Mill and I presume that is how they met. When I was young, Peebles was a mill town. At lunchtime the streets were full of men in their overalls going away home for their lunch. The mill horn blew in the morning and again when it was time to go back to work. Even when we were married in 1953 and got a flat in March Street, the mill horn went at 8 o'clock.

Sheena Dickson remembers her childhood in the shadow of one of the mills:
My father was manager of a tweed mill here. You know where the swimming pool is now? Well, there was a textile mill there. My father

was there as a very young man but he wanted to gain experience and that's why he travelled round, five years here, five years there, but he was so clever that they kept asking him back. That was Thorburn's, and when he came back it was Sir Michael Thorburn who lived at Glenormiston. So they prevailed on him to come back here, so therefore he was the manager then, and he said we should only be here five years but he stayed here for the rest of his days.

We lived near the mill in those days. You know where the parish church is? In front of it, there was an inn. You went down that brae and the house was joined on to that inn, and if you go to it you can still see the marks of the roof. It was never meant to be a house but we lived in it as a house, and on to the house was joined the furnace for the mill and the engine rooms and all the different departments. The men in those days worked on a Saturday as well, a Saturday morning, and on Sunday my father always had the horror that this mill would go on fire. This was an old mill, three storeys high, and the floors were saturated with oil so if he caught a man smoking, he used to say, 'I don't mind you having a smoke, but go outside'. So therefore on a Sunday he and I used to go right down the mill and open all the doors – steel doors between each compartment – and he used to pull them apart and push me through and I thought the mill was spooky when it was quiet and the machines weren't moving. Then he used to explain everything to me – the carding flat where the wool goes in and comes out softly spun, and then it went upstairs to the spinning flat to be spun into yarn. Always he used to explain everything to me, and when I was older he used to say, 'Oh Sheena, if you'd been a boy, you'd have been a great engineer'.

I knew the whole process of making the yarn. There were only a few women working in the mill in those days. The rest of the mill was over in what they now call Damcroft which was Damdale, that was the name of the mill, Damdale, the other half that belonged to the same mill. After the yarn left Tweedside Mill, it went over to what my father called 'the other side' to Damdale, and then it was woven into tweed. There were dyers and designers there, and that's where the main offices were for the mills. They had their own painters and joiners and engineers. In Peebles more or less everybody worked in the mills or on the farms.

My father knew the whole works. He was called a scribbling engineer. He knew all the processes. The managers in some of these mills would not do any work; they would just go round and tell the men what to do. My father used to do things himself and he wouldn't ask the men to do anything he couldn't do himself. In the end, in 1964, there was the fire that my father feared.

Arthur Crittell remembers the night of the mill fire:
There were three mills, there was one in March Street, one in Damdale and one at Tweedside by the Parish Church where the swimming pool is now. In 1964, Tweedside was burnt to the ground by a fire and there were fire engines from all over the borders, including Edinburgh, and men fought all night to bring the fire under control. It lay empty for some years, and then they built the swimming pool and they built Damcroft and the mills more or less disappeared apart from March Street. It changes the town.

Mary Johnstone looks back over the years to her first job in the mill:
I left school at fourteen, I left on the Friday and started work on the Monday, in Thorburn's Mill at Damdale. I had various jobs. I started on the ingiving[1] – we called it ingiving. It was giving the appropriate threads of yarn to the drawer who, in turn, drew the thread through the weaving loom. You were in front, and you gave the thread to the drawer who pulled it through the wee holes. And it started away at the Tweedside Mill and it came to our mill, and if it was to be dyed or anything, it was always dyed at the dye house at Thorburn's Mill.

Fig. 10: Damdale and Damcroft Mills by the Cuddy dominated the town. The cattle pens in the railway yard in the foreground were moved to Clark Place when the station was extended.

---

[1] The ingivers were paid a regular wage; this was a job for newcomers to the mills. But the drawers were on piece-work. Therefore it was necessary for the ingivers to keep up a steady pace.

Then it was spun. If it was to be double, it was twisted. The warpers worked on it in a great big warp mill and we got it after they had warped it. Then we got it and there were bankers, and it was like a great big bank thing, and they put in all the colours. They got the pattern of what was to be done and they put it in so it could go into the weave at the pattern mill. The weavers had the shuttles that went back and forth – they were dangerous things and there were no protections on the machines in those days.

Jean Thomson recalls how she and her friends found jobs in the same tweed warehouse:

I started work at Lowe Donald's, that's become Warwick Woollens.[2] Most of our class left school and all the girls in our section in third year had their photograph taken together because a number of us were leaving and some were staying on and we thought it would be nice to have the year all together. One night May, that's the girl who used always to be my partner, said to me, 'I've got a job at Lowe Donald's and they're still advertising tonight in the Peeblesshire.' I told my mum and dad and I went along and applied and I got one too, so that was May and me both with a job, and then the next week it was still in the paper on the Friday night, so May said, 'We should speak to Leila,' so we told Leila and the three of us all started there.

It was a big tweed warehouse and there was an office in it. They bought in bales of cloth and sold it in cut lengths for suits all over the world – Hong Kong, Japan, Argentina – we used to have an office in Argentina, and we had an office out in Melbourne. Maybe they would export some wool here to be woven and we would export it back as tweed.

I worked first in the office, the place where they sent out the patterns. An enquiry would come from a customer wanting a suit length – they'd like a grey colour and maybe a small check – and you'd look through the pattern book and decide that would maybe do and that would maybe do, and you'd send off the patterns and the prices to them, and they would make their order or not order as the customer wished. When I left there, I was working a wee printing machine. This was after the take-over and there were about half a dozen different firms connected with it. The printing machine printed the tickets with all the different firms that were used in order to stamp the numbers of the cloths sent out as patterns.

---

[2] Now Holland and Sherry.

There were many other jobs to be done in Peebles which our contributors told us about. Because she wasn't a boy, Sheena Dickson couldn't become an engineer, so the family discussed possible jobs for her:

My grandmother was a teacher, she was a great teacher, and the family wanted me to be a teacher like her. But I was always so shy and I said, 'Oh, please don't make me a teacher. I couldn't stand up and tell others what they should know,' so my father said, 'All right, what would you like to do?' I said, 'Well, I like sewing and I like French.' He said, 'Fine, something you can do all your life.' So I was duly sent to be an apprentice dressmaker, at Anderson's, you know Castle Warehouse. In my day it was just a little draper's shop in the Old Town and it had a workroom, a really primitive workroom with a stove, an old stove, and it was my job to light it in the morning. The irons were old flat irons, you know, you put them against the stove to heat them. I started in 1937, I'd just have been fifteen, and I got 4s. 6d.[3] a week.

Willie and Sandy Euman remember their first jobs:

Willie: At Kingsland, I got the exemption to go into the Post Office. I was only thirteen and I desperately wanted to stay on at school, but a job opportunity came up and I went as a messenger at Peebles Post Office. I went everywhere by bike. My longest journey was Manor Head and they seemed infuriatingly to get numerous telegrams, and there was always a charge over three miles, they called it porterage, and I always remember for Manor Head it came to 4s. 6d. It was sixpence for every mile, and that was quite a lot then. It used to pain me to have to ask. My opening gambit was always to wait for someone to pay and most people got to know. There were other distant places – Glenrathope, Kirkhope, Posso. Of course there were not so many telephones then, you see, so the telegram was the thing.

Sandy: Well, I couldn't get an apprenticeship – apprenticeship was the thing in those days. I couldn't get an apprenticeship but I worked with the Buttercup Dairy Company for about a year. Just about the start of the war. I got a job in the printing, the *Peeblesshire Advertiser,* I thought I was going maybe to make a career in printing but unfortunately a lot of older apprentices went away to the war and their jobs had to be safeguarded so they weren't taking on any more apprentices. That was the time I went to woodcutting for a couple of years cutting prime larch, Scots fir and spruces on 365 acres of Cademuir. This timber was much valued at the time, wartime, quite a lot was for pit props, the mines were hungry for pit props.

---

[3] 22.5 pence.

Carrie Ramsay worked at an auctioneer's office, and she remembers an unusual visitor to the town:

I worked where the Castle Warehouse is in Northgate which at that time was auctioneer, valuer and house manager, whatever. After the war there was buying and selling again, and auctions, and I was in and around all the main big houses and small houses for that matter. There was everything there because you had furniture, furnishings, children's stuff. We had a french polisher, an upholsterer, men who did removals, men who did tapestry. Then there were the big auctions, in the town and then we went round doing auctions for when they were selling up a house – very valuable sales at different times.

I can remember, we had an exciseman – he was here in his office. We had a house sale and I had to go along to the site to get receipts and check everything to make sure that the sale was still on – it must have been in the early 1950s – and we actually had an exciseman in the town. I had to go along there and get all the documents and we got a firm in Edinburgh and in the next three months it was all signed and sealed. We went through and catalogued everything and then came back and checked it all out. Not so long ago someone rang me about that and I said, 'Oh yes, there was an exciseman....'

An exciseman was a collector of excise duties imposed on home-produced commodities and services until they were largely replaced by Value Added Tax. As a government agent who assessed and collected revenue, an exciseman was not always the most popular of local officials. Carrie clearly had Robert Burns' poem in mind.

> The deil cam fiddling thro' the town,
> And danc'd awa wi' th'Exciseman,
> And ilka wife cries, 'Auld Mahoun,
> I wish you luck o' the prize, man.'
>
> The deil's away wi' the Exciseman,
> He's danc'd awa, he's danc'd awa,
> He's danc'd awa wi' the Exciseman.
>
> We'll mak our maut, and we'll brew our drink,
> We'll laugh, sing and rejoice, man,
> And mony braw thanks to the meikle black deil,
> That danc'd awa wi' the Exciseman.
>
> The deil's away wi' the Exciseman, etc.

There's threesome reels, there's foursome reels,
There's hornpipes and strathspeys, man,
But the ae best ere came to the land
Was — the deil's awa wi' the Exciseman.

The deil's away wi' the Exciseman, etc.

The firm of Grandison, Plasterers, has been in Peebles for several generations. In its earlier days, it was concerned with the extraction of sand and gravel, as Leonard Grandison describes:
I think what happened was that my grandfather going for a walk on a Sunday afternoon saw the deposits of sand and gravel up at Neidpath Castle. He must have thought about it and approached the Earl of Wemyss and they made an arrangement that he could take as much as he wanted for £10 a year. So he built a boat, I think it was a punt, and he started to bring down the gravel and sand. Probably about two and a half tons at a time was about as much as they could manage. I think it was a job for I don't know how many labourers and a couple of guys quietly going to do it. The stuff was brought down and taken off where Cuddy meets the Tweed, a place which we call the boat-hole. The Cauld was there at that time, and the boat was actually moored up where the bridge goes over to the car park. I think there's still a hook in the wall where it was attached. The first boat for one reason or another was damaged, but the one in the picture was the second boat and it ran on till 1939 because father once took me up when they were filling it with sand and gravel and I got a lift all the way down. During the war, I don't know the story properly, but there must have been a very high flood and the boat either got pulled away or damaged and that was the end of it.

But not the end of it for Sheila Laurie or Mary Johnstone, who have memories of trips on the boat. First Sheila:
Under the bridge over to the Gaffey lay a long flat boat which belonged to Grandison, Plasterers. This was poled up the Tweed to beneath Neidpath where they collected rough sand for their use. Oh for the days of Grandison's footpathways! Occasionally the men would take us the length of the Cuddy in the boat – but never in the Tweed.

And Mary:
We had the sand boat on the Cuddy – aye, that was Grandisons – and the men went up Tweed and got sand and came back. And they used to take us sometimes, they would take us along a bit in the sand boat right up to the steps where the boat stayed – just twenty-five yards or so.

Fig. 11   The Sand Boat on Tweed in the 1920s.

Leonard continues with the serious work of extracting sand and gravel:
The way they worked it is quite interesting. They dug the gravel out of the down-stream side of the gravel bed next to the bank and put the sand and gravel on board, and that left a sort of almost a little channel with water in it, and the next flood that came along filled it up again. Providing your extraction rate wasn't too high, which obviously it wasn't, it was regularly filled up and it would go on for ever. Before the end of the war, the gravel business was dying away. You get the coarse stuff for making concrete and the fine stuff was sand. In fact somebody said to me that they regarded part of the success my grandfather had with lime plaster was in using this coarse sand which was more beneficial for a lime plaster. You can get very fine sand which goes too hard.

Grandfather did all the plaster work at the Hydro when was rebuilt after the fire in 1905. They tried to get the fire brigades down from Penicuik and Edinburgh but the only message they could send was by the railway telegraph, morse code, and the guys who knew morse code were off duty so the message wasn't received till the next morning. But father, who was about six years old at the time, told me that all he could see was just flames over the tops of the trees – mind you, the trees weren't as tall as they are now.

The plaster work was a big job for grandfather. They did the outside harling as well as the inside plastering. Some of the old men who were working with us when I started had obviously been very young men or apprentices at the time it was being done. There's been a lot of continuity in the families who work for us. I myself never had any doubts that I would go into the business. There was a family called Miller. Well, there were three Davey Millers. At one time we had Davey Miller Senior, Davey Miller, Davey Miller Junior. Davey Miller Junior, now dead, would have left school at fourteen and he went to be a pageboy at the Empire Cinema.[4] This lad, his father was a labourer, his grandfather was a labourer, and he was obviously very keen to be with us. He was an excellent plasterer in his day, but he didn't start his apprenticeship until he reached sixteen because plastering is quite a heavy job for a young lad, so father would never take on apprentices until they were about sixteen. Actually a great-grandson - his mother was a Miller, he's called Tommy Wynn - he's working with us still. Then there was a big family of Holnesses. Jimmy was the oldest one and he was placed in the international plaster competition which we entered.

In about 1922, father fixed the mosaic in the War Memorial. He didn't do the actual cross in the middle, I think that came with all the mosaic already on it, but the three panels at the side, he did those.

Ken MacOwan describes how he and his brother came home from the war to take over the family jewellery and clockmaker business in the High Street:
So when my brother John and I were demobbed, we went into the business. My father retired and John and I took over and we were there until we both retired. John did the buying and the jewellery and sales, and I did the clock and watch repairs – I'd been serving my time for clock maker before I joined the airforce. At first we were pretty well absorbed in trying to get the business on its feet and of course we were very dependent on visitors and holiday people coming to the town and Christmas as well. We had somebody to work for us. My father employed a watchmaker named Robert Young who worked in a wee workshop down below street level - it was an old prison but that's all been changed now of course. Then Robert Young left and we had Willy Graham. He stayed with us for a long time until he started up on his own in the Northgate. We employed Jean Kerr as shop assistant at the same time as Willy was the workshop assistant and they eventually married.

---

[4] See page 69.

Margaret Jack stayed on to do Highers at the High School and decided to be a cookery teacher:
In those days we didn't get to have a say because if you were in the top class you did French and Latin and Physics and Chemistry, but I thought it would be wonderful to teach Cookery, because I used to smell the lovely smell coming from the Cookery room and think, 'Oh, it would be wonderful to teach Cookery,' so I trained to be a Cookery teacher. In fact I don't think I was very good at Cookery. I managed to get through the training and I taught it for quite a number of years. I started off at Innerleithen, which was a Junior Secondary in those days, up to fifteen, and then I went to West Linton and Broughton. Then after a year in Edinburgh I go a job at Peebles High School and was at the High School for almost thirty years, teaching, but I actually got promoted to be a teacher of guidance so I didn't do very much cookery after that.

Guidance is really sort of a glorified social worker, as you might say, because you had to look after the welfare of the children and you were the liaison between the parents and the children and if there were any problems you had to deal with them, just guiding them really. But we did a little teaching as well in those days. We were the first guidance teachers really and still did quite a heavy teaching load as well. All the time I meet people who say, 'You used to teach me at the High School,' so I kind of hide when they tell me that.

I think at school English was probably my best subject. I often think I should maybe have been an English teacher, but the one thing about teaching cookery, although there were some really problem pupils, they all enjoyed cooking and you never really had many problems with them. And one reason why they liked it was we maybe charged them 30 pence for making twelve to sixteen rock buns, and they would go out at four o'clock and they could sell them at 5 pence each. And then of course we had all the boys as well. Quite a few of them became chefs. In fact the boy who is the chef in Lazels at the Hydro, he was a pupil of mine, and the chap who is the manager in the Dining Room at the Hydro, he's a former pupil. I don't know if I taught him but he's certainly a former pupil of the High School.

Arthur Crittell's father and grandfather worked for the Parish Church:
My dad was a church officer in the Parish Church for forty years and my grandfather before. I found a letter when my dad died written by my grandfather's employer when he was going after the job as church officer. It said that he was a very find upstanding man and that he would do the job proud. He collapsed and died the back of the church in 1944, I think it was.

My dad used to go on a Friday night to start the fires for a Sunday morning in the winter with a collie dog. He went down one Friday night, a very windy night. He went down into the stoke hole. There were two furnaces and in the middle of the two furnaces was a door which opened up and there was a half-moon tray for water to humidify the church. In the middle of the night, he could hear the wind roaring and the two furnaces were going and everything went very calm. Then suddenly there was a blow back; both furnace doors shot open, flames shot up the stoke hole and the doors shut again. And as quick as he could look, the dog was gone, the dog was back at home. The dog had taken off and he never ever would go down the stoke hole again, never go down to the furnaces. My dad could carry him there, but he would jump out of his arms and come back home.

The fire up there was fired by coal – coke. He went on a Friday night to start the fires, go back on Saturday morning to bank them up, go back on a Saturday night to put more coal on them, and go back on a Sunday morning to make sure they were OK for the Sunday morning, and hope the church was warm enough and if not, put a bit more coal on.

Bessie Johnstone's family worked in a variety of trades and occupations:
My father was a plumber and my mother never worked because she stayed at home. In those days women didn't work when they had families. But there were a lot of war widows and they worked, mostly in the mills, which was interesting for us because we saw them going out and in, day by day. That was Ballantynes. My uncle worked in the mill as a woolsorter, getting the wool ready for the looms. When my dad came home from the war, he took up his old job as a plumber with Fairbairn – they had a workshop in Damdale, where Damdale Mews is now. Afterwards he worked with the Town Council at the town's gas supply workshop on Greenside near the mill in the town – that's where the baths are now.

I think at that time early on, at the mill you only got one day Saturday holiday. You didn't get the holidays they have now. But my dad got a week's holiday and got paid for it. We were really quite lucky, and had my uncle working too. I always remember that for birthdays and Christmas we always got something new to wear. There were other families that weren't as well off as that, as you can see from school photographs.

At fifteen I went to serve in the chemist's shop and I was there all my life. There were four chemists in the town when I started to work. There was Sinclairs where Boots is now, The Medical Hall was always there, there was McDougalls across the street, and I started to work with Sanderson, which was beside The Tontine. At that time there was the Poorhouse up where the

County Buildings are. I remember when I started to work, we had a list of things so long, managed by the county, to take to people at the Poorhouse and I had to deliver messages there. So I delivered milk and codliver oil up there and I can remember the smell and thinking that's what poverty must smell like.

I was working for Sanderson, and then Harry Urquart took over, and then I was still there when Walter Davies took over, and then I went part time across at The Medical Hall, that was until I was seventy – part time for the last five years. I did my four years' apprenticeship and then my mother took ill and I couldn't go away to complete my training, but I never regretted it. Mother was ill for four years before she died. I was still shy and going into the shop was the best thing for me, especially a chemist's shop. Nowadays it's a soulless thing but we knew everyone's troubles and we'd put their names on the slate if they wanted to see the doctor, and it was Dr. Gunn then, and he used to come in there and talk to us.

Dr. Gunn is remembered by many Peebleans, as we shall see later. Dr. Andrew Ramsay recalls his arrival at Peebles and tells how the medical services were organised at that time:
I came to Peebles in 1971 from a rural practice at Pathhead to join Dr. Alistair Paton as assistant with a view to partnership in one of the two practices in Peebles. Dr. Paton was a very forward-thinking doctor, the first in Peebles, in April 1963, to move his surgery some distance from his home to rented premises in Northgate, where the Peeblesshire News office is now; Dr. Wilson and Dr. Stewart soon followed his example. After twelve years, both practices transferred to Hay Lodge Health Centre where they are still based, the site having been bought in 1953 in what was a forlorn hope that it would be one of the first health centres in Scotland.

Since those early days, the way the practice works has changed unbelievably. Then there was an enormous quantity of home visiting, compared with today. I reckoned to make between ten and fifteen home visits during a normal day's work. Then it was easy to drive to any address in Peebles and park in the road close by. As I went on my rounds, I would see the postman, the milkman, the road sweeper, and many other of my patients and could therefore honestly boast that I knew the occupations of most of my patients. The home visits gave great insight into the home circumstances and way of living which is missing now that almost all patients go to the health centre to see the doctor.

Lindores Bed and Breakfast, on the corner of Young Street in the Old Town, was a doctor's house, built by Dr. Clement Gunn, and later Dr. Hamish Stewart bought it and practised from it. There you can still see the two front doors, one for the house and the second for the surgery waiting room. I still remember seeing speaking tubes at doctors' front doors. A night caller would blow into the tube to alert the doctor in his bedroom that a patient needed him.

Appointments systems originate from about the late fifties. Previously at surgery times, patients let themselves into the surgery waiting room and when the doctor was ready, he opened the surgery door and called, 'Next!' At Pathhead I introduced appointments to the surgery in 1968. Each session with a patient lasted longer than today's five minutes, and after we had discussed the reason for the patient's visit, our conversation would range more widely.

The geographical boundaries of the practice stretched eastward to Velvet Hall, northwards to Leadburn, westward to Stobo and Drumelzier, with some patients in the earlier days from Broughton. A doctor would try to do all his visits in one direction on the same day; Dr. Wilson had a routine of going up Manor Valley and up Tweed valley regularly on Tuesday and Wednesday afternoons. But the necessity of emergency calls often resulted in long drives by day and by night (though not so long as from my Pathhead practice where I once drove during a day over Soutra to Lauder, up to Haddington, before coming back via Dalkeith to Pathhead).

By occupation, the greater number of our patients were agricultural or mill workers, of both sexes. In former days outlying patients, especially from farms, would frequently travel to the surgery, by private means if possible. As time progressed, more households had cars and more patients were working in a variety of jobs in Edinburgh and commuting to work each day.

Patients nowadays are so much better informed with access to the internet. I am sure this must make a practitioner's life much more difficult, just as the advent of antibiotics made my life easier. One of my compatriots, in his youth, had his tonsils removed on the kitchen table, and a fellow practitioner incised a quinsy throat on the same useful solid piece of furniture. Nowadays if anything were to go badly, a doctor could be up in court. In conjunction with the great advances in medicine in recent decades, this makes the job of today's doctor more demanding than my work in those days.

The two practices in Peebles each were made up of two partners, each with about 3,000 patients. Our wives were very much part of the practice, taking calls, providing secretarial support at weekends and after 5 p.m. weekdays and from 12 – 1 when the secretary had lunch. Their husbands had to pay them because the NHS did not pay for wifely secretarial help. Dr. Paton employed a secretary from 9 till 5, but we did alternate nights on call, while our wives also took calls on alternate nights as well as at lunchtime. Today there are still the two practices, but each has three full-time doctors, one part-time doctor and a trainee registrar, as well as secretarial support fully paid by the NHS.

Peebles Nursing Home down by the river was originally Peebles War Memorial Hospital, with about 20 beds. It opened after the First World War as 'our hospital', formerly two houses one of which was called Morelands, a name still recalled by old worthies. Consultant obstetricians and surgeons visited weekly in turn to carry out minor operations such as sterilizations, hernia repairs and ligations of varicose veins. For emergency obstetrics, a 'flying squad' could be summoned by phone from Edinburgh. I remember one emergency after a birth when I expected the maternity 'flying squad' to arrive within half an hour but they took one and a half hours; fortunately the patient was saved. Cottage hospital and home deliveries were a most satisfying part of practice. But it was a great relief when the baby was crying lustily and the mother was well and on the whole I was relieved when the obstetrics unit in Peebles was closed.

Arthur Crittell comments on change in the medical services:
The other side of Tree Bridge was Dr. Paton – the surgeries of doctors then were all in private houses. Dr. Temple's was the house facing Coronation Street, and you used to go in and along the corridor in his house and into a small room which was his waiting room. He had his surgery in the front of his house and when he had finished with a patient, he shouted, 'Next!'

There's been a lot of progression over the years when the doctors changed the hospital and moved from the War Memorial up to Hay Lodge. They had four doctors in the town and now they have ten and they still can't cope. I don't think the hospital's big enough for the town. Now they have an Ambulance Station which they never had before.

Jean Thomson remembers the four doctors in the two practices with respect and affection:
Where Somerfield's is, a doctor's surgery used to be there, old Dr. Wilson. You went up the drive and there were like two parts, and the first door at the right hand side was leading to the surgery and the house was on the left hand side, and then the garden to the back went right down to the lane. A doctor was a doctor then. He would come out and see you and would come out at any time of day or night. That was Dr. Robin Wilson, but before my Dr. Wilson, his father had been a doctor in Peebles as well.

And then there was Dr. Stewart. He stayed at the top of the Old Town, in Lindores. And then going along Greenside, nearly at the boat hole, up the steps was Dr. Thom's house, and again he had his surgery next door. And then Dr. Temple, across Tweed Bridge, the big house that faces you, that was Dr. Temple's house. If Dr. Wilson was on holiday and anything happened, Dr. Stewart would come and vice versa, and the same arrangement was between Dr. Temple and Dr. Thom; someone always covered. The doctors knew you and they knew your family and they had an interest in the families they attended. It's nice to know that back then you had four doctors who looked after everyone.

Of course, the conversation between Peggy Ferguson and Mary Johnstone got round to medical matters, so they can have the last word:
Peggy: You remember Freda McLean? Well, we were playing rounders and we were all standing in line waiting to get our turn with the bat, you see, and Freda missed the ball and it hit me, and I was carted off down to the doctor. She missed the ball – and it was a hard ball – and it went full on my eye, and I was carted down to Dr. Wilson's surgery and he put clips in, it wasn't stitches. The doctor did all that in his surgery. There was no chasing off to hospital. His surgery was in the Northgate. That house was a beautiful stone house, where the supermarket is, and it was demolished. If there's anything I hate, it's seeing a beautiful stone-built building demolished. Dr. Manson and Dr. Martin took over and there was another doctor, tall and handsome, wavy navy, they took over that practice.
Mary: Then there was Dr. Paton, and Dr. Wilson.
Peggy: You see, long ago families had their doctors, and it was so funny because if you married, your husband had one doctor and you had another doctor, and when doctors came here first they couldn't understand how it was that a wife and a husband had a different doctor. It was just that your family had had a doctor, you see. You could change if you wanted to, but then you were used to him. My mother always had Dr. Wilson.
Mary: The Mitchells at the Kingsmeadows gave up their house as a maternity hospital in the war. After the war was finished, they offered it to them for a hospital and they wouldn't take it. It would have been an ideal hospital, the grounds and everything were beautiful.
Peggy: The pregnant women came from Glasgow and the cities. They came for three months to have their babies here.
Mary: Yes, because of the bombing happening in Glasgow then. And they got up earlier than we did because they had to travel home. We could lie for nine days but they only lay for a week. My nephew was born there and my youngest son was born in the hospital here.

Peggy: It was up to you whether you had your baby at home or in hospital. When we were in the mill, we joined our nursing scheme. I think it was just about sixpence a week or something, and we were taken to hospital at Tweed Green – that was the War Memorial hospital which Earl Haig opened. But you had to pay if you were in, you see, so we were in this sort of insurance. It was a lot cheaper because I remember I was in when I had my daughter and I got quite a bit off the usual price. But my mother had five of us all at home and all with the midwife.

Mary: Well, I had Ian at home but then my mum was with me.

Peggy: Just the midwife, there was never a doctor there – but she was lucky, she never had any trouble.

Mary: But they did huge big operations in that War Memorial hospital. There was the tonsil day. There were two at the top and two at the bottom. I was at tonsil day with Ellen – you remember her? She was at the top of the bed and I was at the bottom of the bed, they had that many.

Peggy: Well, they just cleared the place and made that tonsil day.

Mary: You were taken in the morning and home again at dinner time.

Peggy: I was kept because I haemorrhaged. I was kept for a week afterwards, but it was all right in the end.

Mary: When they made it free, it was the biggest mistake they made, because everybody went and got teeth and glasses and everything.

Peggy: I think it was abused at first. That was one thing about our younger days – we didn't abuse things.

Chapter 5

LEISURE TIME AND BELTANE

Even though the working day was long and holidays few, Peebleans found time to enjoy themselves. We asked people how they spent their leisure time, especially when they were young working lads and lasses, without the responsibility and cares of young families. We found that they led busy and enjoyable lives which they look back on with pleasure.

Bessie Johnstone describes how she was always active:
After work in the evenings I went skating, roller-skating. My friend who worked in the library and I used to skate home at night. And we were all dancing-daft of course. And then of course you could go to the pictures every night in Peebles if you wanted to. If we didn't go dancing on Friday nights, we went to the pictures. Of course we got skating in the winter time. They flooded the parking space on Kingsmeadows Road and it froze in the winter and you skated there. We cycled and we walked – we were never still.

Pam Fairless describes her main leisure interests:
I joined the Tennis Club. I walked from Eliots Park to the courts and played tennis. In those days, you weren't allowed in if you were a junior after 6 o'clock. I can remember once being invited to come and watch and thought it was a great honour to watch after 6 o'clock.

I went to Peggy Weatherson for music lessons. I went on a Saturday morning and I've a lot to thank her for. She loved music and through her I've got my great love of music. My father played too, and we played a lot of duets together. Peggy Weatherson was a founder of the Music Club which was up in the Picture Gallery in those days. Edith Warton, who came during the war to stay up at Venlaw Castle, was a concert pianist and her career was knocked off course because of the war. She taught Peggy Weatherson, and Amy Barratt as well and they got really enthusiastic and then they started the Music Club.

Up in the Meldons was a great place for picnics. Gypsy Glen was another place I used to like to go to. That's what's called a drove road and it would take you away up the hills. Everyone walked, and you'd meet and walk in the park as well. We were lucky with parks. At one time, where the Victoria Park Centre is built, there was a pond[1] which froze over in winter and there would be skating there.

Dancing and cinema were Jean Thomson's main recreations:
There was plenty for teenagers to do in Peebles. After we started work, May and another friend were keener on dancing and Leila and I by that time were more interested in theatre and we used to save up for ballet companies coming to Edinburgh. When we were teenagers, there were two picture houses, three changes at the Empire, two up at the Playhouse, and there was dancing on a Friday night and a Saturday night at the Drill Hall. So there were plenty of places for young folk to go and there weren't people hanging about the streets as you find now.

Carrie Ramsay remember the cinemas too, and also the balls at the Hydro:
After the war was over, when things got back to normal, we had all the big balls again, the Young Farmers, the Tennis Club, all these things had their different functions, all in their evening dresses, it was lovely. And sitting in the ballroom at the Hydro I remember at three o'clock in the morning having bowls of soup, it was lovely.

At one time there were three cinemas; there was the one in the Briggett[2], the Empire, owned by the family called Scott. I remember going along to the Empire – sixpence to get in. Eventually Mr Scott died and there was nobody in the family to take it on, though the Scotts apparently had cinemas in other places. And then the Playhouse, in the High Street. And occasionally, though I never went, in the Burgh Hall they had films – who ran that and what was going on there, I really don't know.

But luckily Ken McOwan does know!
Aye, at the back of the Chambers Institute was the Burgh Hall, of course the cinema, aye, we used to go to the cinema there on a Saturday afternoon, tuppence to get in and a penny to spend. Silent films used to come on and there was a man playing the piano. I can remember Willie Robson was the pianist, he lived up Gibson Place[3]. Balcony at the back, which cost, I think, sixpence. All the nobs used to go up there and we were in the fleabox down below. Then they did Gilbert and Sullivan and the like – I remember Pooh-Ba; the character in The Mikado was played by John Lyon, a local solicitor, and he did the part very well. It was great. That was quite a thing, the Burgh Hall.

---

[1] The Curling Pool.
[2] Bridgegate, alias Empire Brae.
[3] This was Pam Fairless's father.

Sheena Dickson remembers family music sessions:
Music was a great thing in our family's life. I had piano lessons and when I got to High School I'd do half an hour's practice before I had my tea and then the rest of the night was homework and I sort of got away with it. And when I was at the High School, we went to dancing classes too. The teacher came from West Linton. You know Whities? Well behind there is a hall that's now made into a bookshop and that's where we did dancing – French, Greek on your bare feet, and the one I liked best, Highland dancing – sword dancing – I was good at that. You wore pumps for that, bronze-coloured dancing pumps.

There was always music in our house because my mother was a great pianist. When we came home from the dancing class, she'd say, 'Well, what did you do today?', and we'd tell her, then she'd play the piano and we'd do the dancing. My mother had two brothers who were violinists. One of them played the music for the background of the silent films and then, when they finished at night, there was an ice cream shop here called Toni's and they used to go in there and he used to say to them, 'If you play, I give you supper'. Then we'd go along at night-time to my grandmother when she lived here and we'd just sit in the firelight (there was only gas but I don't even think it was on) and my mother played the piano, the brothers played the violins, my father played a mandolin and then we'd all sing songs. My father seemed to like Irish songs, though he was Scots, and we always sang the *Londonderry Air* and *Kathleen Mavourneen.*

Sandy Euman's young life was full of music too:
I suppose we were fortunate, we participated in most things, football, golf, hill walking. The lifestyle's changed completely, people have no time now, hurrying and rushing about. They don't seem to have time to do things. Our other interest was piping, we grew up in a piping house – bagpipes. Father was a great teacher, playing the violin too as well as the pipes. I just stuck to the pipes. I've played the pipes for a good seventy years round Peebles and the Linton district, sometimes in front of hundreds of people. It was in the Innerleithen Pipe Band, and solo piping too. Father always said how lucky he was to have had a good teacher and he always tried to give the best teaching to his pupils and took them right up to pibroch. Innerleithen Pipe Band has been in competitions in recent years, doing very well. Cut-throat business, the pipe band competitions.

The Tweeddale Society had been founded in 1913. It held lectures during the winter and organised excursions and walks in the summer. Bessie Johnstone was one of the younger members of the Tweeddale Society during the 1930s. She particularly enjoyed the Victoria Day Excursions which commemorated Queen Victoria's birthday, 24 May:

They were all day trips by char-a-banc, starting at 9 o'clock in the morning. They were on Wednesdays, because that was half-day for all the shops in Peebles. We went one year to Oban, and another year to Sweetheart Abbey. Another trip took us to St. Andrews and Crail and then we had lunch at the Marine Hotel at Elie. There was no road bridge then so we went on the ferry from Queensferry and I remember it was very cold on the crossing. I used to go with my friend Winifred from the Library. My brother Robert and my Uncle George, my mother's brother, came with us to Sweetheart Abbey and my mother came to St. Andrews.

The minute book of the Tweeddale Society contains a report of the outing to Sweetheart Abbey which took place on 25 May 1932:

> The members and friends of the Tweeddale Society, Peebles, had a most successful outing on Wednesday (Victoria Day). The party numbered seventy, this being easily the largest number who have taken part in these annual excursions. The outing on this occasion was to Dumfries and Sweetheart abbey, and when the Abbey was reached, the party inspected the ruins of what must have been a truly magnificent building when it was intact. The lunch hour was spent in Dumfries and thereafter the return journey was commenced ....
>
> Peebles was reached at 9.30 p.m., just twelve hours after leaving. Everyone greatly enjoyed the outing. The day was rather dull, but the rain kept off until the company was well on their way home.

Fig. 12 Members of the Tweeddale Society at Marine Hotel, Elie, 25 May 1935. Bessie (right) and Winifred are sitting on the ground at the front.

Carrie Ramsay remembers an old custom:
Then again, different ways. We had great fun when the young people were getting married, because we used to lay them out on the office counter and black them. They didn't have wild stag nights like they have now. We had whole lots of hot water so they could clean themselves up one way or another. That was a north country custom, actually, north country being Angus and Aberdeen. It was great fun, great fun!

Church-going and church-based activities played a big part in our contributors' lives and in these accounts we hear of them from the users' points of view. Sheila Murray describes the range of leisure activities available to occupy the infrequent holidays, and the choice of churches:
People worked hard and there were few holidays. Millworkers had one week's unpaid holiday in August, one day in October, one day in April and two days at New Year. Work continued as usual on Christmas day. Life was not all work, however, and there were plenty of activities going on – cinemas, concerts, sport, YMCA, library, three tennis courts, a thriving Philharmonic Society and church activities. People were more active and took more exercise. There are some lovely walks in the countryside around Peebles and most people went for a Sunday afternoon walk. There was plenty of local talent to entertain us. Several excellent singers entertained us at concerts in the winter evenings. The actor, Bill Crichton, who lived in Peebles, often performed at these concerts and Anna Buchan recited Scots poetry. Special groups such as the Women's Guild, put on plays.

There were three Presbyterian churches in the town – the Parish, the Leckie and St. Andrew's at the foot of the Old Town. St. Andrew's Church was an attractive building, adorned inside with beautiful Kauri pine wood from New Zealand. St. Peter's Episcopal Church, the Leckie and the Roman Catholic chapels still occupy their original sites but St. Andrews was demolished and the congregation linked with the Leckie. All churches were well attended and in the Parish there was a large Sunday School and Bible Class. Next to the railway, at the foot of March Street, was a Mission Hall called the Railway Mission[4] where services were held, and there was also, near the end of North Street, a Salvation Army Hut. The Salvation Army preached and sang hymns at the Cross in the High Street on Saturday evenings.

---

[4] Established by Mr John Sked, the Mission was housed in 'The Tin Kirk' built at the junction of March Street and Edinburgh Road in 1902. In 1960 the name was changed to Peebles Gospel Mission and services continued until 1982. The building was demolished in 1989.

On Saturday evenings we went to the Band of Hope in the Parish Church Hall where Halyrude Court now stands. Here we signed the pledge eschewing all forms of alcohol. People of all ages went and it was a real fun evening. Those of us who had some talent, however small, took our turn at providing the entertainment. On other occasions we had guest speakers or perhaps a lantern slide show.

The Railway Mission was the one that captured a lot of interest and there are some vivid recollections of what went on. Ilene Brown recalls Christmas at the Mission:
The Railway Mission was at the Sandbridge foot of March Street, beside steps up to Dean Park. Now Brown's car showroom takes up this site plus ground which was a shrubbery. The Mission was a corrugated iron building with a wood stove for heating – it was very cosy. Many children went every Sunday to the Mission and were taught bible lessons, and learned passages never to be forgotten. Christmas time was wonderful. A large tree was covered with gifts unwrapped so one saw trains, trumpets, dolls, bears, cars. There was great excitement as you wondered what toy had your name on it. A piano was played and many hymns learned. The wonderful people in charge were Miss Sked, Miss Jessie Ferbuson and Mr Tyndale Leithbridge.

Jean Thomson remembers the words of one of the choruses:
I used to go to the Railway Mission. It was a big tin hut and we used to go there and sing hymns and choruses. One was 'Climb, climb up sunshine mountain with faces all aglow.' Another one was
> Sunshine corner, oh, it's very fine,
> It's for children under ninety-nine,
> All are welcome, every seat is free,
> Peebles Railway Mission is the place for me.

Bessie Johnstone went to the best that was on offer at several churches:
We went to St. Andrew's Church and we went to the Band of Hope – it was magic lanterns we got there and we made the pledge, 'I promise by the wrath of God to abstain from all intoxicating beverages and drinks until the day I fall asleep.' We went to the Parish Church Sunday School because they got dancing at their party and we didn't get dancing at St. Andrew's. There was another, what we called the Tin Church[5], at the foot of March Street. We used to go there at Christmas because they had a bigger Christmas tree.

---
[5] The Railway Mission.

Peggy Ferguson and Mary Johnstone share their Sunday experiences – not to mention dancing days! :

Peggy: When you started day school, you went to Sunday School.

Mary: I went to the Band of Hope, at the Parish Church Hall. They had a wee scout hall and then they had another hall you could make in two, and they had a great big hall. It was just a way of religious life, it was something like a Sunday School. When you went out the door, you got a wee text to learn for the next time. Then we went to Sunday School, and then we went to Bible Class and then we went to the Church.

Peggy: Did you ever get tests at the Sunday School, bible tests? Because my older sister, she was the only one that got her certificate framed because she had 100% for the questions about the bible. I had 87%, and my certificate wasn't framed.

Mary: There was a wee test but there wasn't an examination for who was the best. After the Bible Class we all went up to the cemetery gates and my brother played the accordion and we all went, after we'd been to church, and danced.

Peggy: We were quite adept. I used to slip down to the Drill Hall. I loved it.

Mary: Wednesday and Friday and Saturday.

Peggy: Aye. It was an awful job having enough money. It was ninepence a time on a Saturday night. Later on, I took up Scotch dancing. I've got my certificate. And then we had a Girls' Club.

Mary: The Girls' Club was always held at the Vestry at the Church.

Without a doubt, the high point of the year for young and old in Peebles was, and is, Beltane. There is plenty written about Beltane and the planning for the next Beltane goes on throughout the year, recorded in the local press and widely advertised. We were fortunate to collect the memories of Margaret Jack who rightly told us, 'I'm quite an expert on Beltane!' She tells the inside story of her experiences in Beltane:

I was really very lucky because I happened to be the 50th Beltane Queen in 1949 so of course it was a very special occasion and I got lots of lovely presents from everybody and all the previous Beltane Queens were invited for the day and invited to lunch. The luncheon was in the Tontine, but the Queen and the court were not invited. My aunt, who was Margaret Veitch, who had been the Beltane Queen in 1920, she was there and all the previous Beltane Queens were there. It was a beautiful day, but it was very very hot, and I fainted at the War Memorial. However, my aunt, who was a nursing sister, saw me sway and ran across and managed to catch me in time before I landed on the pavement. The Crown is quite heavy, but the sceptre is really very heavy, and on a hot day, and with the excitement and not having had very much to eat …. And you have the train as well, that's heavy too, though you have the pages to carry it. But it was a great day, it really was a wonderful day, a day that I shall never forget. I had over sixty telegrams that had come from all over the World. The First Courtier was Bobbie Boyd – he's now Dr. Robert Boyd, a Professor in some University in Canada, who's much brainier than I was, and he got the Dux Medal.

Fig. 13   50th Beltane Queen, Margaret Jack, and Court.
Crowned by Miss Isabel Whinthrope, daughter of the 1st Beltane Queen, Margaret Muir.

Lots of my family as well as my aunt have been principals in the Beltane over the years. My father's cousin, whose name was William Watt, was the Cornet in 1902, my great-uncle Robert Watson was the Cornet in 1904. My uncle was Cornet in 1924. My brother George was the First Courtier in 1935 and my brother Bob was the Cornet in 1951, two years after I was the Beltane Queen. When my brother was the Cornet, his Lass couldn't come so I had to go and dance the reel with him.

Fig. 14   Robert Jack, Cornet 1951, leading the Riders past the Old Parish Church.

In those days, there were three dances on the Friday night, there was a dance in the Drill Hall, there was a dance in the Old Parish Church Hall and there was a dance at the Burgh Hall, and we had to go round these three dance halls and dance the Eightsome Reel.   And by the end of it you were exhausted.   Mind you, I was very fit in those days.   And I hate to admit that fifty years since I was Queen, they invited me to crown the hundredth Beltane Queen.   The highest honour Peebles can bestow, I think, is to invite you to crown the Beltane Queen.   I am one of an exclusive club of two, Sheila Murray and myself, who are the only two Beltane Queens who also crowned the Beltane Queen.

As Crowning Lady, you help judge the Fancy Dress Parade on the Friday night, and you have to go to everything.   From the opening ceremony, you're treated like a VIP, especially on the Wednesday night when you're taken up to Neidpath to see the Warden introduced, and then you're taken into the Castle for the drinks and the ball – it's a great night – then dropped down to see them fording the river, and then you're driven up to the Golf Course for the parade and of course all the Principals have a car space as you're always parking – it's great fun!

On the Saturday afternoon before, we have a lunch at the Hydro, all the Crowning Ladies. And the Crowning Lady Elect is the Guest of Honour. We have a special room at the Hydro and it's the most beautiful lunch, it really is a lovely afternoon. And the Crowning Lady Elect is presented with her brooch. But as well as that, there is also another brooch which Colonel Sprot gifted for the Crowning Lady as a presentation for Lady Hay, who was Colonel Sprot's aunt. I think Lady Hay was given the beautiful golden brooch by the Town Council in commemoration for her gift of ground for Victoria Park and Colonel Sprot gifted it back to the town to be worn by the Crowning Lady at the crowning ceremony. So we all wear this lovely brooch.

A lot of hard work is put into the preparations for Beltane, which I don't think people realise. The ladies on the Committee nowadays spend about the whole year sewing costumes and repairing costumes. The costumes have greatly improved since my day. Then they were all stored in mothballs and brought out each year and they weren't nearly as nice as they are now. I was a Tudor lady and a Victorian lady and a Dutch girl. I think they were about the only three things I did because during the war the children weren't dressed up.

When I was Captain of the Guides, we used to put a lorry in the parade. You couldn't get the lorry until four o'clock at night because of course they were in use and I think the judging was at half seven but the lorries had to be ready by half six. So you have about two hours in which to decorate the lorry and it was murder, trying to do it. We only put a lorry in twice, I think, because the work was so hard. You really need strong men to do it. The girls find decorating it terribly hard and they would be all dressed up to go in the lorry.

Rev. David MacFarlane recalls his participation in the Beltane ceremonies:
I was generously invited to be the Warden of Neidpath in 1984 and that I did count as an honour because I always felt it was important that the Parish served the whole Parish and not just the congregation and the links between the community and the Kirk I thought were important. I was grateful to be invited to be the Warden of Neidpath as I had been the Warden of the Cross Kirk on several occasions.

As Warden of the Cross Kirk you had basically to conduct a service for the opening of the Beltane on the Sunday, at the Cross Kirk, which was always a very pleasant occasion. You were always regretful if it had to be held in the Parish Church because the weather was not kind. With the help of the other clergy of the town, you conducted that service and gave the address for the occasion. As Warden of Neidpath, well, we always jokingly used to say that you had to get a brush to clean out the Castle but that is not quite true. Your main duty was to make a speech to the community and to the group that travelled up to Neidpath Castle on the Wednesday of Beltane, that was your principal duty. After that it was purely an honorary appointment and involved nothing in practical terms. During the Beltane, on the Friday night, ex-Wardens, former Wardens, had a dinner in one of the local hotels and occasionally at Neidpath itself, and we invited the wives of Wardens.

Bessie Johnstone remembers her Beltane costumes and a sad end to her Beltane involvement:
I was a fairy, I was a gypsy, I was a milkmaid, I was a knight in a black cloak decorated with stars and moons. When I was a fairy, I took the wings home and dad, being a plumber, did something at the back and fixed them somehow. I don't know what he did but mine were the only ones that stayed up till the last. I was going to be a Georgian lady and go in a stagecoach, but I took jaundice and I nearly broke my heart. I had my costume and it was green and yellow, and I was the same colour! First time in my life that I was off school. The Victorian ladies and the Georgian ladies got to go on the stagecoach and I actually had the costume and I took jaundice. I was twelve and I went to the High School, and that was the end.

Pam Fairless recalls the excitement of the Beltane:
When I went to Kingsland, of course I was in the Beltane. They had an Advanced Division at Kingsland where you went on till you were fourteen in those days, so the queen was fourteen. I think it was nicer when the queen was older, I think it looked better.

Everybody went to everything in those days. The fair came and it was down in Cuddy Green. Everybody wore the Cornet's colours. At that time the Cornet had his colours and a tie was made and all the men wore the Cornet's tie for the Beltane. Everyone tied flags out; when we were in Eliots Park, we had two big Union Jacks, and my father always tied them to the gate posts and everybody had flags out. The houses were all decorated, just the same as they are now, if they've got a Principal living in them. We went out to see the horses – not nearly as many horses as there are today. I would say there were maybe eighty, something like that, just all the local people who had a horse. In those days, too, the Cornet's Lass didn't ride a horse. She just turned up in beautiful outfits every night, with different hats and dresses for different evenings. She just bussed the colours, she didn't ride at all.

Everybody went to the concert which used to be held in the Parish Church Hall that's no more, where Halyrude Court is. There was a big Parish Church Hall there and you couldn't get a seat! They had to turn people away it was so popular. It was in the days of tenor, bass, soprano, contralto, accompanist and a compere and maybe an elocutionist, and they had solos, duets and quartets – a right old-fashioned concert. I sometimes wish they would have it again because it was good, it was nice. In those days they wore evening dress. I've even been an accompanist before the Parish Church Hall was knocked down, and you wore your evening dress and then men had on their dinner suits to sing and it just added a touch of class to the concert. So that was the Beltane, that was really the great excitement.

Jean Thomson recalls how Beltane ceremonies went on despite the war:
I'd gone up to Kingsland School and they'd taken on the Beltane during the War. The first year, the crowning was in the playground and it was Sheila Murray – of course she didn't have a very good crowning. She was asked to crown the queen after fifty years, that was 1990. And the following year, 1941, the queen was crowned up in Hay Lodge Park and from then on it took place in the afternoon. They brought a special platform for them in Hay Lodge Park, and it was a really hot Saturday. I remember, a friend and I queued up to get a threepenny treat. All the school children got a ticket and you got thruppence, which was quite a bit in those days.

I never dressed up because all my Beltanes were during the war. From 1942 to 1945, the crowning was down in the cricket pavilion up in Whitestone Park, where the Rovers play football. And 1946 was the first crowning back on the parish steps and Muriel Gilchrist was queen that year. And the children were in costume again.

A very wet Beltane sticks in Sheila Laurie's memory – but it didn't dampen the enthusiasm:
The Beltane was the highlight for the children. The excitement when costumes were handed out! The thrill when the Queen was announced at the school! The thrill of Beltane morning when we had to be at Kingsland by 8 a.m., 7 a.m. if you were requiring face-painting. We set off to walk to the Church Steps, down Rosetta Road, March Street, Northgate and so along the High Street. In my day only the Cornet and his two supporters turned out that day. Mostly the weather appeared to be good, but the year I was a Poppy, we only got on to the steps when the downpour started. So

bad was it, the parade was cancelled. I had red dye through my hair plus all my vest, pants and socks were ruined. Needless to say, our teacher gave us a rollocking on Monday. No wonder she was mad – only one girl brought a costume back whole – they were made of crepe paper!

The Shows were held at Greenside and consisted of Swingboats, Cake Walk, Helter Skelter, side shows, lots of stalls, coconut shies, shooting ranges and Try Your Luck, flinging rings over articles which if you were lucky you won. Oh the lovely music, the lights and hustle and bustle of the shows! We were not allowed out late but Jean and I had a window from which we would watch until we fell asleep.

Chapter 6

PEOPLE AND ORGANISATIONS

and Hedgehogs

Our contributors told us of many people and interest groups in Peebles that were of great significance to them and to many other Peebleans. We have included as many of these as we have space for in this book. There will be many other people and groups that you could tell us about, but we hope that the ones we have included will be of interest to many readers.

There have already been in earlier chapters some references to Dr. Clement Gunn, so we shall begin with two more comments about him.

First from Sheena Dickson:
I was born in Peebles in 1922 in my grandmother's house on Greenside. There was a famous doctor called Dr. Gunn. On that particular day, Dr. Gunn and Field-Marshal Earl Haig were to get the Freedom of the Royal Burgh of Peebles, so I decided to be born precisely at 11 o'clock, so Dr. Gunn said to my grandmother that I upset his apple cart.

And from Bessie Johnstone:
I remember going with Dr. Gunn when he went up to the Manor Valley Sanatorium at Barns. The matron was a Miss Peyton and she had a peke dog called Peter Pan Peyton. Dr. Gunn used to take my friend Wendy and me up to the Sanatorium and he went in to see to his patients while we walked up the valley and back, and then had a cup of tea with him. Then he brought us back down. He would take us up there on a Wednesday afternoon because Wendy was in the Library and I was in the chemist's shop and that was our half day. He had a big open car from Tweeddale Garage and he used to drive down to Wendy's house to pick us up.

Dr. Gunn lived at Lindores which he built. He called it Lindores because that's where he met his wife, skating on Lindores Loch. He died in 1933; it's a pity his memorial is not very well kept. You can hardly see anything on it now, you have to go really close to read it. My nephew put a wee bit in the paper at the time, and he put a bit about Clement Gunn Square. As he said, 'My name is going down in history!'[1]

---
[1] He was called Clement Gunn after the doctor, see p.19.

When Dr. Gunn's memoirs were published in 1935, the Foreword was written by John Buchan, soon to become Lord Tweedsmuir. In his autobiography, John Buchan recalled his childhood summers in the Borders and recorded that his father's family had long connections with Peebles. His mother stayed in Peebles in her old age, near her daughter Anna and her son Walter. Anna was herself a novelist, writing under the name O. Douglas, and Walter was a leading lawyer in Peebles and both were prominent in the cultural life of Peebles.

James Renwick remembers the family:
I remember Anna Buchan as a very gracious lady. She did a lot for charity. We had a shop at the bottom of the Old Town and I remember she used to come in every Christmas and order half a dozen of these decorated tea caddies to be sent to various people, most of them old-age pensioners, but it had to be anonymous. On no account had we to reveal who they came from. And Walter Buchan was the same – he donated a lot to charity but always anonymously, and I know this because my sister used to work in his office as a typist.

Anna Buchan used to get asked to the various guilds, Church guilds, you know, and she was very good at giving recitations. One was 'The Broken Bowl' and the other one that I can remember was 'The Next Stop's Kirkcaldy' – you know, the train. I always remember the last words: *'I ken mesell, with the queer-like smell, that the next stop's Kirkcaldy'* – Kirkcaldy being the linoleum town. Those were her two favourite pieces and I remember when she brought an old bowl along and at the end of the poem she smashed it to the floor. She was a very gracious lady and she was held in very high regard in the town.

Walter, he was the Town Clerk, and a very efficient Town Clerk too. He was a Cornet at the Beltane in 1920 and he was the Warden of Neidpath in 1933.[2] Anna, she crowned the Beltane Queen in 1922 and was also Warden of Neidpath in 1937. Lord Tweedsmuir, that was John Buchan, he was Warden of Neidpath in 1935. I always remember him coming because he was one of my favourite authors and it was of great interest to me when he was Warden of Neidpath. And his son, the next Lord Tweedsmuir, was also Warden of Neidpath in 1958 and Lady Tweedsmuir, his wife, was also Warden of Neidpath in 1967. She was MP for Aberdeen and very active in politics.

Amazingly, Walter Buchan was Town Clerk of Peebles from 1906 to 1948 and in all but one of those years read the Proclamation of the Beltane Fair and the Burgh Bounds.

---
[2] More about Beltane in Chapter 5.

The book of minutes of the Tweeddale Society from the revival of the Society in 1913 until its suspension during the War in 1941 shows that Walter Buchan throughout the whole period served as Honorary Secretary and Honorary Treasurer.[3]   John Buchan is recorded as having addressed the Society on four occasions, twice during the First World War and twice in the 1920s.   Anna Buchan presided at meetings at least once.   Dr. Clement Gunn was an Honorary President from 1923 to 1933.

Jean Thomson has memories of the Buchans too:
Our next door neighbour, Mrs Cumming, used to work for Anna Buchan in the mornings, when she lived in the Bank House.[4]   Once or twice, at Christmas, Mrs Cumming gave mum and me a book by O. Douglas and had her sign it for us.   And one time – this is quite funny – I had a piece of the king's birthday cake, but I think I only had a crumb of it.   It was like this: George VI and Queen Elizabeth (that was the Queen Mother) were out in Canada visiting John Buchan who at that time was Lord Tweedsmuir and Governor General of Canada, and the king's birthday was while he was there.   Lord Tweedsmuir sent home a piece of the king's birthday cake to his sister who gave Mrs Cumming a small piece of it, who brought it in and divided it among five of us!
    When Anna Buchan was away on holiday, Mrs Cumming used to go and stay in the Bank House to have someone there and I can remember one day being down in the Bank House with my mum visiting Mrs Cumming and we were in the sitting room having a cup of tea.   Now whether we should have been there or not, I don't know!
    And her brother, Walter, he was the lawyer when my dad was exchanging houses, and because the house he was buying was more than the house he sold, he had to borrow an amount of money to bridge the gap, and he complained so much, not about paying the money back, but about having to pay interest on that money to Walter Buchan!

No one coming into the centre of Peebles can fail to be impressed by the Parish Church towering above the High Street on the hill where once stood a castle.   Rev. David MacFarlane recalls taking up his ministry at Peebles in 1970, following periods of service at Dunblane Cathedral and in Aberlady:

---

[3] See the account of a Tweeddale Society summer outing on 9.71.
[4] In the High Street, on the corner of Cuddy Bridge, partially demolished for road widening at Cuddy Bridge, until recently Hopscotch.

We had a congregation in Peebles, on paper it must be admitted, of something like 1300 people when I came in 1970. Now there are about 700 on the roll, and of course it's such a gloriously large church that when you see the congregation scattered around, you can see the gaps, but nonetheless, it's a great place, Peebles, with all its traditions and history.

I sadly never met my predecessor, James Hamilton, because he had died before I came. I was profoundly grateful to him, because he had set up so many organisations within the church and within the parish in Peebles that I leant on heavily, and I will be ever indebted to him for that. My organist, who was then Ian Cruikshanks, for whom I had a great affection, showed me orders of service and James Hamilton had timed how long the first hymn lasted, how long the call to prayer lasted, and it was itemised and I think if it was ten seconds longer than it should have been, that ruined his weekend. It was literally timed to the second, and that was typical of James Hamilton's meticulous organisation.

We had the Women's Guild which was quite a large organisation. It was a fairly mature group of ladies and there were about fifty of them came. They were very active and the congregation was dependent on many of the things the Guild did. They were always called up to do this, that and the next thing and unfailingly did that, and it was a great sadness to me to hear that the Guild had closed. I was old-fashioned in that I was hesitant to introduce ladies in the Kirk Session, although two ladies were ordained to the Eldership in my ministry.

There were many more weddings than I gather there are now, about fifty or fifty-five a year, and we had something approaching eighty funerals a year when I was minister. They weren't all congregational funerals but they were rightly Parish funerals. And the task of looking after the bereaved folk was a job in itself without visiting the whole congregation which you still tried to do.

When I came to Peebles, we made many changes in the church building itself. For example we built in the side aisle the small chapel in memory of James Hamilton, my predecessor. His associate and helper at that time was Kenneth Grant and the furniture in the side aisle was put in in his memory. The screen which shows the history of the Parish was erected in the side aisle which was set aside as a place for smaller services. We also extended the main communion table, we rearranged the chancel with the 5 originally in the chancel and put them in their present place in the crossing, we introduced the Book of Remembrance, and the stalls which were moved from the crossing were given cushions to make them more comfortable. The organ console was taken from the chancel into its present site in the south aisle and it was extended to three manuals. I must admit I regret that we couldn't put in a central aisle – not for the beauty of weddings only but to enhance the church.

Other kind additions in my time were the windows in the vestibule, created by Crear McCartney. Colonel Sprot very generously gave the Hay Window and one of our Elders, Albert Black, gave the Beltane Window, the one with the horse and various parts of the town that are used for the Beltane ceremony.

In my time, the churches began to speak more readily to each other, which was only sensible. The ecumenical movement has increased through the years, and in Peebles it was no exception. We had a very happy relationship with the principal churches in the town, the Baptist Church, the congregations of the Church of Scotland, the Roman Catholic church, the Episcopal Church all combine happily and not least in issues such as Christian Aid which is a common concern of all churches. In my time we started the annual joint service where the churches gathered in the Parish Church to worship together.

James Renwick describes the present day Guildry Corporation of Peebles, an institution which dates from 1647:
Today, the Guildry is made up of fifty members who are elected because they have really done something for the Town. We meet twice a year, have a dinner in the Hydro once a year, and attend to any matters of local importance that are brought to us. The old Guildry goes back to pre-council days when the local town council was made up of the various Guilds in the town. It used to have just twelve members but then the number was increased to fifty. The front pew in the Gallery of the Parish Church belonged to the Guildry, and we have the tradition that the Sunday following the dinner we go to the Church and occupy our pews in the front row of the Gallery.

I have been a member since 1952 and I am the oldest member. It's all men, though once we had a lady speaker – she was the Sheriff. One of the traditions we have is that on the night of our dinner, we always have a pie sent to the ladies of the house for their suppers. It is delivered from Forsyths to all the different wives, so that the ladies have a pie to keep them company when we're away having our dinner.

Rev. David MacFarlane reflects on the Civic significance of the Parish Church:
The Civic Service started again in my time, with the help of the then Provost, as I was keen on the link between the town and the Parish Kirk.

In the back gallery of the Parish Church you can still see the stalls which latterly became the province of the Town Council, and the one which is more elaborately carved was the Provost's chair where he sat on civic occasions when they attended the Parish Church. In my time when local government was rearranged and the Provost and the Town Council ceased to be, I remember conducting the final service.

The people who sit up there at the annual service now are the members of the Guildry Corporation. Now you are invited on to the Guildry Corporation, as I kindly was, as a kind of honorary body. They have no authority and are a group of some fifty men in the town who are business or people of esteem in the town. You're invited to become and once a member, always a member.

Isabel and Duncan Taylor recall the time before Peebles lost its town council:
Isabel: We had people in the town then that were totally different to now. We had councillors that ran the place and loved the town. If you wanted something done, you only needed to ring them up or go and see them at the Tontine, the place they all used to gather. And the solicitors used to be there on a Saturday morning, and a lot of things were discussed about what could be done to help. And things got done. A solicitor would tell you, 'Oh that can't be done like that, it's against the law,' but a lot of things were done and it was all voluntary.
Duncan: If you wanted something done, it was done in the social club on a Sunday morning. That was another place the councillors met, Sunday mornings. Several old women went to the Tontine on Saturday when their door was broken. If the problem was not solved when they came to the Tontine, they were told to meet in the social club on the Sunday morning.

Aidan Sprot explains about Tweeddale and describes the highlight of his tenure as Lord Lieutenant of Tweeddale:
In the old maps, the names Tweeddale and Peeblesshire are interchangeable. A dale is always the high bit of any river system; Tweeddale is the high bit of Tweed Water. When I was on the old County Council, the Peeblesshire County Council, and right at the end of the old county council days in 1974, we were asked what should be the names of the new regions which were the Border Region and the county which was called the District. I said I thought the big region should be called The Borders because it's always known as The Borders, and our new District Council should revert to the old name of Tweeddale. After all, Peebles is in the Royal Burgh's name, and Tweeddale is a far more attractive name and historically is very

important, so that when they did away with the county councils, it reverted to Tweeddale. And I was appointed Lord Lieutenant of Tweeddale but my predecessor, Sir Robert Scott, was Lord Lieutenant of Peeblesshire, and it was exactly the same area. I was Lord Lieutenant for fourteen years until I was seventy-five.

When the Queen is in Holyrood, she usually visits a county, and I kept writing to the Palace saying it's high time the Queen came to Tweeddale. She came when I was a Deputy Lieutenant in the late sixties, early seventies, and I thought that, come the eighties, it was time she came again, and eventually she came in 1988. I made a programme covering the four centres, Peebles naturally, West Linton, Broughton and Innerleithen and then she went on to Melrose to open the new Borders General Hospital. At West Linton I had people to meet the Queen who would be of interest such as breeders of Highland ponies, and at Broughton it was fairly similar – sheep dogs and blackfaced prize tups. At Peebles we had a display in the Burgh Hall of about twelve different stands. I remember the Curling Club had a stand with some of their trophies on it and pictures of when they curled on the Minny[5], which is that bit of river just above the Cauld, when it froze over one year. And then we gave a lunch in the Hydro which was hosted by the Regional Council. And then she went to Innerleithen and we had a similar thing in the big hall there and showed her various things about the local mills and their cashmere products. Then we said goodbye to the Queen and she went to open the Hospital. So that was our great day. That was the highlight, obviously, of my tenure as Lord Lieutenant. Otherwise Lord Lieutenant is more or less a name more than anything else. He's a useful person, because if something needs to be done, he has a bit more clout. You can say, 'The Lord Lieutenant wishes something done.'

Jean Phillips records the beginnings of the Girl Guides in Peebles as well as her own involvement with the movement:
It was only after I had become District Commissioner for Guides in Peebles in 1983 that I discovered that the first ever Girl Guide Company in Scotland had been formed in Peebles. Lady Erskine of Venlaw House, who was the wife of Rear-Admiral Erskine who had at one time been an ADC to Queen Victoria, formed this Girl Guide Company because her daughter, Veronica, very much wanted to become a Girl Guide.

The Peebles Girl Guides were formed and registered in February 1910, that being the first company registered in Scotland. Agnes Baden-Powell, the then Chief Guide, wrote to both Lady Erskine and to Veronica, giving

---
[5] Minister's Pool, see p.7.

encouragement and advice, and both these letters are in the possession of the local archives. There is also in the archives a signed photograph of Agnes which she sent to Veronica.

The Guides met in Venlaw House. They were taught bandaging, first aid and the usual things that Girl Guides in the early days did. They were taught to swim at the Hydro, which Lady Erskine must have arranged for them. One of the Company, Nellie Borthwick, received a medal for bravery for saving a young lad from drowning while on holiday at Aberdour. During the First World War, Venlaw became a military hospital and the Guides went there and made bandages and did chores round the hospital so they really were serving their country.

In 1985, during my time as Guide Commissioner, the 75th anniversary of the first Guide Company was marked by a party at Venlaw. The theme of Guiding at that time was to try to spread the light of Guiding, the idea of Guiding, to the young people in our community, so we took a lamp and Alistair Cummings, then owner of what was by then the Venlaw Hotel, put it on the ramparts, and for that night, the light of that little candle glass lamp would be seen from Peebles – it was the light of Guiding shining over Peebles. I hope that in a few years' time, which will be the hundred-year anniversary, that people will do something similar and take the light of Guiding back to Venlaw.

Fig. 15   Guide Commissioner Jean Phillips and Alistair Cummings hold the light of Guiding at Venlaw.

The other thing that I did during my five-year spell in Peebles was to try to make the units much more ecumenical. I felt that since we had Guides from all the churches in Peebles, we should do the same as the Beltane Festival did with the Warden of the Cross Kirk and take our thinking-day service round to all the churches. Unfortunately we didn't get quite all round them but we did have one very nice year in the Parish Church. I felt it broadened the girls' horizons to go to other people's churches and also no one felt left out because we hadn't been to their church.

Rev. David MacFarlane remembers the Boys Brigade:
It was always the Boys Brigade in my ministry. We started the Girls Brigade with a first class leader who still leads them. The Boys Brigade in my time was shared between the Old Parish and St. Andrew's Leckie Church. The Boys Brigade was always the official Church organisation. It changed through the years in that latterly a congregation could sponsor either the Scouts or the Brigade, but the Brigade was the original Church organisation.

And Arthur Crittell remembers Boys Brigade officers and camps:
Sam Ferguson was a great Boys Brigade man and all year he put cans away for the Boys Brigade camp. By the time of the camp came round, a lot of labels had fallen off the cans and they didn't know what was in them. They were making mincey pies and they opened a can and put the contents into the pot, and they discovered it was rhubarb!

The Boys Brigade camps were very good, very well done. There were two Boys Brigade companies at the time, and there was also a Scout troop, all very well supported, all connected to the Church, yes, St. Andrew's Church, Leckie Church, the Parish Church, they were all connected to a church. The First Company of the Boys Brigade was part of St. Andrew's Church and the Second Company was part of the Parish Church. The Parish Church captain was Walter Denison, and it's still running, and Sam Ferguson was the captain of the First Company, the one where Alec Hammond the painter was an officer.

Bill Goodburn is a true gutterbluid, as he tells in his account of his life and career as a lawyer, based in Peebles since 1963. His account, which he dictated to his computer, contains so much of interest, from police cells to sheepdogs, from the Sheriff Court to the Tweeddale Shooting Club, that we offer it to you in its entirety:
I was born in the nursing home on Tweed Green in Peebles on my mother's birthday in 1939. This does qualify me as a true Gutterbluid. Peebles at that time had changed little over the past 40 years. It was still a somewhat

parochial border town with a population of 6000 people mostly employed in the tweed industry with a society that was about to be torn apart and changed forever by the Second World War. My father went off to war with the Royal Air Force and spent two years in West Africa. The only enemy action I saw during that time was firing my pea shooter gun at a stray Heinkel bomber which had wandered off course after a bombing raid on Glasgow. Towards the end of the war, my mother and I became camp followers as my father was then running what is now Prestwick airport and we had digs in Prestwick. The greatest supposed treat at that time that I remember was the arrival of a strange looking fruit which was green and yellow and curved and was placed on the sideboard to ripen. It was the sole survivor of a bunch of bananas which father had sent from West Africa! The sad thing was when it finally became ripe I really didn't like it!

We returned to Peebles in 1946 by then I had attended three little schools and was not acceptable in Kingsland with a non-local accent nor did I have large tackety boots which could produce hordes of sparks on the tarmac. Some hefty scuffles and the adoption of the local dialect reduced the bullying. I remember a very mixed bag of teachers many of whom were very kind but discipline was certainly much harsher than at present times. The Lochgelly Special (or "strap") was frequently used on primary pupils. The boys had outside toilets without a roof and the competition was to see who could pee over the toilet wall. My father resumed practice as a lawyer with Blackwood and Smith W.S. W.S. stands for 'Writer to the Signet' which in these days signified, or was supposed to signify, an above average standard of lawyer and has nothing to do with swans . It required that you served your apprenticeship with a Writer to the Signet who ultimately confirmed you were a suitable person to practise law, having passed the necessary exams. Then the Keeper of the Signet applied the royal seal and you were launched. Modern requirements meant that you had also to become a member of the Law Society and the body which administers all solicitors.

At the end of primary school I travelled for two years to school in Edinburgh by train to the Edinburgh Academy. However this proved rather an exhausting commute and I finished my schooling at Peebles High School. Thereafter I went on to Edinburgh University to complete a Law degree. The degree in these days reflected the much more general education which a solicitor was thought to require in his role as "a man o' pairts" in that the student began with a general Master of Arts degree with only three Law subjects, including Latin as lectures in civil law were delivered in the Latin up until 1955! The LL.B. degree, which contained all the technical subjects, was only over a two-year period whilst you were serving an apprenticeship in a legal office. This has now been replaced with a degree which lasts a minimum of four years in full-time study and covers many more subjects reflecting the growth and complexity of the Law over the last fifty years. Apart from the pleasures of student life and the joy of meeting my wife the most exciting thing which happened during my university career was learning to fly with the Royal Air Force Volunteer Reserve. This gave hours of flying pleasure in later life and led to the building of an aeroplane in retirement, altogether another story!

After deciding not to remain as a lawyer in Edinburgh I returned to Blackwood and Smith in 1963. It was quite a change to come back to the country after a specialised role in High Court practice with a large firm Tods, Murray and Jamieson. The first job I was asked to do was to export a champion sheepdog to the United States. This was the first of several belonging to a well-known sheepdog trainer, J. M. Wilson. His customers in the States often spent a small fortune on telephone calls to acquire the correct whistle to work their dogs properly. There were three legal firms in Peebles all associated with their respective banks and my senior partner Alexander Fyfe was the last joint bank manager lawyer in Scotland when he retired aged 82 in 1965. The office is situated above what was the British Linen Bank at 39 High Street. It was built in 1870 and designed to provide not only the bank but offices for the lawyers and living accommodation for the lawyer-manager and until 1965 the firm enjoyed rent-free accommodation. After the retirement of Alexander Fyfe, the firm bought the premises. There were whistle tubes as on an old steamship connecting the offices and the bank so that the senior partner could literally whistle up the bank manager. It is also interesting to note that until 1936 the majority of the county council affairs were administered from the same office by about three people including the county's finances and at that time one of the partners, John Ramsay Smith, acted as county clerk.

When the new County Buildings were opened in 1936 John Mackie, who had carried out the County Council business, moved to the new buildings as a full-time civil servant and County Clerk. Education alone was run by another law firm, Thorburn and Lyon, and the roads surveyor operated from the Sheriff Court building. All a startling contrast to the enormous administration required by present-day local government. The firm can actually trace its roots back to 1672, but it has existed as a partnership since 1839. Before the Second World War much of its business was connected with the factoring of large estates and farms. When I joined in 1963 most of this business had gone but there was still a core of factoring work. The junior partner always looked after the Court business which included serving on the 'Poors' Role'. This was before the days of Legal Aid and each law firm undertook the task of representing criminals, who could not afford a lawyer, free of charge. Monday morning usually produced a crop who had to be visited in the grim white tiled cells at the back of the police station (long since out of use as too harsh and Victorian). Many of these criminals had offended as a result of too much drink and they were sorry sights without ties, belts or shoe laces and having no washing facilities for two nights. There was also a notorious police sergeant who felt that young and budding criminals were best dealt with by him and they received a good cuffing in the same cells and were sent on their way without due process of law. This may well have been an effective remedy but it was heavily stamped out and could not be tolerated.

The most serious crime I had to deal with was the rape of a three-year-old and I had only two jury trials in 15 years of Court work; one where the accused was charged with being in possession of explosives at the time of the beginning of the Irish troubles. In fact he had stolen the explosives to go poaching. The other was severe bodily harm almost to the point of death by using a broken bottle in a fight. By confusing the jury as to whether my client was right or left handed and the position of the wound I managed to achieve the unique Scottish verdict of "not proven." One of the great skills in Court work was knowing when to stop asking questions. One of my partners had a classic illustration of this and he told the story against himself. He was defending a lady accused of being drunk in charge of her car. This was in the days before breathalysers when the police had to demonstrate that the driver was not fit to drive through a series of tests, for example walking on a straight line, and also on their general behaviour. The lady's dog had taken seriously ill and she had to drive it to the veterinary surgeon in Biggar for an operation. The vet suggested she should wait for the dog in a local hotel where she calmed her nerves with generous portions of whisky and on the way back to Peebles ran off the road at the quarry corner near Neidpath. When my partner interviewed his client she explained to him that she had been putting out the car lights when the police arrived. In Court the police constable duly gave his evidence and my partner asked him what his client was doing when he arrived on the scene, in the hope of establishing normal behaviour. The policeman said she was attempting to put out the lights. My partner should have stopped questioning at that point but he went on and said, 'Do you mean she was sitting in the car switching off the lights?' 'Oh no,' said the policeman, 'She was outside the car hanging the hubcaps over the lights!' - end of defence!

Although Court work could be very intense and involve great emotion it often provided the light relief and laughter. I had a regular poaching client who always left a fish on the doorstep of the old folks' home as an insurance against being caught and the Sheriff never took a very hard line when he heard of this kindness. The Sheriff Court was held every second Wednesday in the delightful building adjacent to the Parish Church presided over by one of the Sheriffs of Lothian and Borders who normally sat in Edinburgh. The most outstanding Sheriff of that time was Isabel Sinclair, one of the first women to be appointed to the bench. She very much enjoyed the friendly atmosphere which existed between the law agents practising before her and built up a great rapport so that she knew exactly when we really felt a mitigation in sentence was justified. Criminal courts were held as required between the main sitting and often presided over by an honorary Sheriff, a job I did for some years in retirement.

The lawyers in Peebles, until the reorganisation of local government in 1975 and later regionalisation, still carried out part-time administrative tasks for example Edward Laverock of J. and W. Buchan acted as Town Clerk of Peebles and part-time Procurator Fiscal. Brian Shaw of Thorburn and Lyon was Town Clerk of Innerleithen and Procurator Fiscal to the Innerleithen Burgh Court. I acted as Clerk to the Licensing Board which dealt with the granting of liquor licences and the opening times of pubs and hotels and I was the last clerk in private practice. We also had several unpaid jobs which were a hangover from the past; for example, I was Clerk of the Peace and in that role I looked after the Justices of the Peace and trained them for taking a seat on the bench in the Burgh Court. One of my partners was Clerk to the Lieutenancy and in that position had to organise, for example, all royal visits to the county and act as secretary to the Lord-Lieutenant.[6] The same partner was also Clerk to the General Commissioners of Income Tax and legal aid representative of Peeblesshire. Gordon Fyfe was also secretary to the Tweeddale Shooting Club which was founded in 1790 and still dines three times each year on grouse, partridge and pheasant in the Tontine hotel which a group of the club members built about 1808 as a "tontine" when they fell out with the owner of the Cross-keys hotel their former hostelry. The last two survivors of the original tontine decided to share the hotel between them rather than wait to see who was the last to die.

Death, moving house and divorce are reckoned to be three of the major traumas faced throughout life and lawyers of necessity are involved in all three. In being able to provide assistance and helping clients through these difficulties made the job seem worthwhile and often established very close

---

[6] See p.87 for a royal visit.

relationships with your clients who in our small town were often friends. It was not uncommon to change completely the direction of someone's life by putting them in touch with the right business to buy or the right house to buy. This close relationship did to some degree change in the 1980s with the rise of consumerism. The public were encouraged to shop around for the cheapest deal and as client loyalty was reduced so lawyers felt less close to their clients and more formal relationships developed with lawyers feeling bound to write more letters to protect their position and note every word said by telephone on the file. Specialisation was also with us and as our partner numbers had grown from four to six so I became more interested in commercial law work, company work, executry and trust work. Life was incredibly varied and I found myself looking after clients as diverse as a national hotel group, a major landowner on Islay, a company pioneering timber frame buildings with sites all over Scotland as well as farmers, garage proprietors and the ordinary folk of Peebles who had a problem that required legal assistance. I suspect I was probably one of the last of the general practitioners of the old style. Strangely at this time we found our client numbers growing as many people did not like to be shifted from one specialist partner to another as they had to do in the large firms to buy a house, float a company or make a will.

By the 1980s half the law graduates at Edinburgh University were female and we had our first lady partner Patricia Watson in 1983. The advent of women into the profession produced a much more balanced and user-friendly society. They made their mark not only in matters of family law but across every field and by 2005 Blackwood and Smith have two male partners and three female. As in every business the advent of the computer produced a revolution particularly in the ease of accounting and record keeping but it also substantially increased the volume of paper. This was followed by the advent of the fax and e-mail which meant a solicitor could no longer expect a four-day respite after the dispatch of a complicated contract to the opposite side. The law required to adapt itself to accommodate electronic mail as part of contract without a signature and this has posed problems of interpretation in court. While Scots Law is a separate system from English Law much of the mercantile commercial and company law has become common so that the old Scots law commercial lease of two pages now follows an English style of sixty pages. The most difficult task facing the present-day lawyer is to cope with the volume of new legislation pouring forth from the Scottish parliament, the UK parliament and Europe. Before the Second World War the statutes passed by the UK parliament would usually be a slim volume taking up two inches of shelf space; now the annual output takes several feet. Specialisation and a reduction of services into the fields in which you are expert is now an essential, so goodbye forever to "the man of pairts"!

In conclusion I can only hope that the present-day lawyers will have as much satisfaction and enjoyment from the practice of law as I did and that they will continue to put the interests of their clients first before any other interest. On the other hand the public will recognise that the legal profession remains the last independent bastion to whom they can turn in times of trouble and be assured that their cause will be pursued without fear or favour. There are, of course, lots of jokes about lawyers but when I was on the public relations committee of the Law Society I carried out some personal research and asked people who didn't know I was a lawyer if they had a good lawyer. 99% said they had an excellent lawyer! That seemed a very high satisfaction rate, I hope it continues.

Willie Euman, ever a strong campaigner for the countryside and for the preservation of wildlife, tells of his one-man war on behalf of the hedgehog, for which he has become deservedly well-known and respected:

I devoted ten years to my hedgehog campaign. It was quite by chance. I'd left Peebles and moved into the country but commuted each day to my job in Peebles. I lived four or five miles out at a delightful spot called Easter Happrew. It was at Easter Happrew one night, a rather chilly night in late March. I was putting out peanuts, first favourite of all birds, for some of my visiting garden birds. I thought, 'I'll give them a wee treat tonight,' but it was pretty late, I should have realised that birds were all gone sensibly away to wherever they go in the early evening and I was late with my peanuts. Lo and behold, I looked out and there was something there. I think I went out with a torch to see something that had attracted my attention and here were four hedgehogs guzzling away at the peanuts. The great thing about peanuts is there's nothing else at night, out during the hours of darkness, other than perhaps the odd mouse, that would eat the peanuts, so they are left to the hedgehogs. I made a great discovery – hedgehogs are absolutely head over heels in love with peanuts.

Well, I began to develop an affinity with hedgehogs and then I realised there was something else – a great menace as far as hedgehogs were concerned. There seemed to be an explosion of what we call cattle grids at farm road ends and estate road ends. This was a dreadful pit about four feet deep with an iron grill over the top. The idea was a good one for the occupants of the estate and the farm because on a wet night when they returned from a shopping mission to Peebles, it didn't mean opening and shutting a gate. You could drive over the grid which prevented animals that might have been pasturing within the road end from straying on to the road. A great thing, but nobody thought about the hedgehogs. It was tailor-made for this wee bundle of spikes which wandered by night. It would come across the bridge, maybe at the side of the road, and then it would slip through into this dreadful pit and there it would remain, suffering a lingering death.

I began to examine cattle grids and, heavens, the hedgehogs, innumerable hedgehogs I rescued. Using a fisherman's landing net which I introduced through the bars on the grid, I captured the hedgehog and with care brought it up through the bars. There was no other way to do it. There was no escape provision for hedgehogs whatsoever. So here was I and of course it brought me into the press and I wrote to numerous wildlife bodies and the major dailies and Sunday newspapers. My campaign was launched by the Peeblesshire News whose editor, Richard Pringle, said to me, 'This is rather a wonderful story. I've been in contact with *The Scotsman. The Scotsman* would rather like to use it. Could I have your permission?' So I said, 'No, I have no objections at all. If it's of interest and hedgehog's a viable piece, please do.'

Well, my name went round the country linked to the hedgehog and I suggested a device that could be easily constructed. I didn't give it a name, it was named for me – they called it the Euman Ramp. There were some made, quite elaborate ones, and I enjoyed wonderful cooperation and collaboration from farmers and shepherds on estates and farmland. Wherever there were cattle grids, they put in an escape provision for the hedgehog and this was rather wonderful. Campbell Napier of Langhaugh, for example, made a beautiful little construction. It even had a little signpost, 'Escape This Way', a little sign on a post, beautifully printed. No hedgehog could read it of course but it was rather wonderful, it was almost like a miniature of a modern highway with all these road signs and all the rest, to the hedgehog's advantage.

Oh heck! It was a constant job. My phone ringing very, very often. Quite often I found people who would love to have a young hedgehog for a pet for their family but I would tell them of course unless they stayed awake in the night-time hours, a pet hedgehog wouldn't be much use to them because they sleep during the day. And one of the most difficult things is to sex a hedgehog. Looking at a hedgehog there's no way telling a male from a female except to hoist the creature up by its rear legs and it uncurls and it's easy then when the areas that usually determine a living creature become exposed.

After some considerable years of all those dreadful pits, autumns and winters came and blown material filled the pits until the situation relieved itself. There was such a pile of flotsam in the pit and they filled up and of course a hedgehog falling in now didn't fall very far and it could easily extricate itself. It's a pretty good climber, the hedgehog. So it became less of a problem. But I continued to look as there were always new pits being constructed. There was some new legislation introduced which I, with great humility, warm at the thought, brought about through my endeavours. Some new legislation went through the House of Commons a propos wild creatures and agriculture so that some provision, when those dreadful cattle grids are put at road ends, is made for wandering-by-night hedgehogs to escape. And this was done. I later examined the cattle grids at Dawyck and many other places, the most recent ones put in place, and to my great pleasure I always discovered that there's ample provision for hedgehogs to escape.

The greatest risk now to hedgehogs is crossing the road. Hedgehog numbers are falling drastically I don't know what can be done about it. There was once a time when a hedgehog even by night could walk across a road and safely get to the other side, but such is the frequency of traffic, there's no chance and many get killed – it's very sad.

Chapter 7

PEEBLES AT WAR

The wars of the Twentieth Century are mentioned in earlier chapters as part of childhood and young adult memories by many of our contributors. In this chapter, more memories of Peebles during the Second World War are gathered together. Many Peebleans had war experience in other places, both in UK and abroad: these we have not included. Peebles itself was mercifully a long way from the danger and destruction of war, as Sheila Murray summarises:

Day to day life in Peebles was not greatly affected by the war. Apart from our young men and women being called up to serve in the forces and the inevitable sad occasions when we learned of casualties, life went on fairly quietly. At first we were inundated with evacuees, mainly from Edinburgh, but before long they started drifting back home again. For a time we had Polish officers billeted in our homes – anyone with a spare bedroom had to take one in – before they also moved on. There was an Italian prisoner-of-war camp in the town. The only time we had experience of bombs was when Clydebank was bombed. Scores of German planes flew over Peebles on a clear moonlit night, and on their return journey jettisoned some incendiary bombs on Standalane Farm. A land mine left a huge crater in a field at Eddleston. We reckoned the German planes were looking for the ammunition dump on Leadburn Moor.

Sheena Dickson describes the effect of the war on mill production, and on her own life:
The war started and my father was churning out khaki, khaki, khaki. He'd work all night and the mill went all night, churning out khaki for the army. There might be just one odd machine with some civilian thing on it. They worked all night and they couldn't leave the doors open or the windows because of the blackout, and sometimes he'd say the heat was stifling. At the same time, my father was in the St. John's Ambulance and I was in First Aid and we were both at the First Aid Post every night. In the blackout I knew all the doors down the old town and the windows and I used to feel down them and then get across Cuddy Bridge and past the parish church and then down the slope to the mill.

I did five years' dressmaking apprenticeship and by this time the war had been on two years. I worked with two women and we never spoke; they didn't speak to me – you daren't look up even though I was quiet. I'd done more or less my five years and one day it had been particularly bad. On my way home, I went into the Labour Exchange and volunteered.

Sheena went into the ATS and left Peebles to have amazing experiences during her wartime service – but that's another story.

Carrie Ramsay joined up too, but kept in touch with events in Peebles:
Then there was the Royal Army Medical Corps, the bulk of whose personnel were stationed down at Glentress. During the war that's where the troops were and they came up daily to service the Hydro as a hospital. You just turned your hand to anything, no matter what your job was. Once our own troops had been moved out, it was the Polish troops who were here, and there were Poles right around the Borders and you find a big number of Polish names in and around the Borders. At that time, Hay Lodge House was commandeered and the Polish headquarters were there.

Bessie Johnstone's brother Robert was in the Territorials, many of whom from Peebles, Innerleithen and Walkerburn enlisted in a revived 8th Battalion The Royal Scots. They were photographed outside The Drill Hall.

Fig. 16 8th Battalion The Royal Scots, Autumn 1939, at The Drill Hall.
Robert Johnstone is in the centre of second row and Bessie's cousin George in the same row, third from the left.

James Renwick enlisted in the Royal Artillery. About forty men of the Peebles Section, 'D' Troop, 228 Battery, 66th (Lowland) Medium Regiment, Royal Artillery were mobilised on 2nd September 1939 and the photograph demonstrates the lack of preparedness for the war. Some men were without uniforms and it was eight months before they were a fully equipped artillery unit. In 1943, they became part of the 8th Army in North Africa.

Fig. 17   Peebles Section 'D' Troop, 228 Battery, 66th Medium Regiment Royal Artillery, outside The Drill Hall. James Renwick is on the second row, kneeling third from the right, with chin partly covered.

Leonard Grandison was about ten years old when his mother was organising entertainments for the troops who found themselves in Peebles: During the war there were canteen concerts held for the troops round here at Chambers Institute, at the Hydro and at Glentress. My mother ran concerts for entertaining the troops and she was quite involved with that. I was always slightly disappointed that she never got any recognition for it. Although lots of people did other things that were far more important, the concerts kept up morale. She used to go round employing some of the local people from some of the concert parties, and she occasionally could get some of the soldiers who could sing or recite something – it was a bit spur of the moment, some of it.

The Hydro was a hospital. What happened at the Hydro was that they would bring in nurses and orderlies and doctors and build up a complete medical unit and then when it was ready and organised, it was sent out to wherever and then they would repeat the process.

I remember as a child being taken up to the Hydro by my father and mother to see Harry Gordon. He must have been entertaining the troops – I think father must have pulled a few strings to get him there.

Pam Fairless was a teenager during the war and has many vivid and precise memories of how life was affected:
I was thirteen when the war started in 1939 and then it was that evacuees all came out to Peebles from Edinburgh and the town was very busy. There was always an army presence in Peebles, all the time. The first regiment I remember wasn't a tank regiment but they had vehicles with caterpillar wheels and they made an awful mess of the roads here. The Hydro was cleared and made into a military hospital and the Nissan huts were put up in Victoria Park and the town just changed completely. Sometimes some of the soldiers' families came, and houses were to let because when men went into the army, their wives went away to stay at home with their parents and they let their house. Soon there were a lot of new people in the town and a lot of Peebles girls married soldiers.

My mother used to go and help at the canteen at the Hydro, on a Monday. And then she used to go another day to help at the canteen for soldiers at the Chambers Institute. If my mother saw what she called a 'poor soul' at the canteen, she would ask him for tea on Sunday. We never had Sunday tea on our own, we always had people that she found. I remember one who had been newly married and had had to leave his wife and was feeling lonely and down. And then the Polish officers came and they were billeted in the town. We had one who was billeted with us who was very anxious to learn English and I used to have to sit and listen to him practising. There was always a joke about me yawning because I was bored to tears listening to him trying to read English. Some of them got the name of chasing the girls, but our one was very serious and very anxious to learn English. He just became one of the family and used to bring his friends as well. My mother managed to feed them, but with the rations we got I don't know how she managed, but she did.

Nearly everyone had a Polish officer billeted with them. There was a big camp up at Crawford and I think they would be weeding them out to see if there were any people who were spies there and then as they were gradually filtered out, they were sent down to Peebles. They were all officers. We had quite a laugh once because my uncle, who was in the office at the Tweeddale Garage, had a Polish mechanic there who was just a corporal, and he put his arm in a sling because if he hadn't, he would have gone along the street saluting all the time. So he put his arm in the sling to save himself.

Some of the Polish people stayed, but our one went away back to Poland as soon as he could. In a way, he was very good for my piano playing. I was playing Chopin, of course, and I can remember us going to Edinburgh with my mother and father and he bought me records of Paderewski playing some of the pieces that I was practising. And it didn't dawn on me till later that it was thanks to him that I had to listen to it and then I had to try to copy it.

I went to Moray House in Edinburgh in 1942. I got the bus at Dalatho at twenty to eight and I got into Edinburgh about ten to nine. The bus was packed with evacuees' husbands, people who'd come to stay out in Peebles, the buses were packed. Some people had to stand the whole way. They had black-out curtains in the bus and if it was the early morning bus, the blinds were down. There were two bits of wood that went into slots down the side of the bus with a black-out curtain which hung down, and then it was rolled up when it was daylight. And, if sometimes there was no room, even standing room, they brought what they called a utility bus, which was a little tin bus with slatted seats, and that was a duplicate – and there were often duplicates.

We all had to make the best of things. We couldn't get clothes, so it made us clever. You had to pay coupons for knitting wool, but you didn't for darning wool, so I knitted a jersey out of a box of cards of darning wool – so you can imagine how crazy it was. I had forgotten all about it until I met somebody years afterward who said, 'The thing I remember about you was your darning wool jersey.' I had another friend who bought two dishcloths and she bought coloured darning wool. She wove it in and out of the holes of the dishcloths and joined them at the shoulder and sides and wore it under her suit. My mother crocheted us handbags out of cord. We did all sorts of things to make the best of what we had.

Has somebody spoken about how the German planes flew directly over Peebles to get to Clydeside? We had a lot of sirens, warnings in the night so we got up and my mother had a theory that you should sit on the stairs because when she saw bombed buildings, the staircase was still there. We didn't have a shelter so we sat on the stairs. There was only one night when they dropped incendiaries and they mostly landed on the golf course. One landed on a farm roof and smoked itself out on the stone floor. I think the cow was sick but that was all. And then a land mine on a parachute fell at Eddleston but it was on marshy ground and didn't really do much damage either. And I think there was one sailed over Venlaw, but that was all that happened, so we were quite lucky.

Jean Thompson was just twelve years old when the war ended but has particular and vivid memories of her 'war work':
My cousin Margaret was in the ATS and was billeted in Edinburgh. She was in what was called the Kinema section. She had a projector and a screen and everything to show films, which they took sometimes to hospitals, sometimes in barracks or wherever the troops stayed. On a Monday, for a while, they would come to Peebles and show films up in the Hydro and then the following day she would move on to Hawick. So when that happened, she used to come and stay at home and if it was the school holidays, I would go up and fetch her from the Hydro and carry reels of films and stuff and I got to see the films. She used to show a film again up at the Hydro at night. She'd have a big truck and my chums and I would wait for her for we knew the time she would leave. And soon we'd be driving down with here. She'd put us into the back of the truck and drive us round about two or three streets through Dovecot and drop us out at the end of Dovecot – it was exciting!

We were in George Street when the Polish troops came to Peebles. Many were billeted in the Parish Church Hall and for some of them, like the captains and lieutenants, they tried to find them room in houses and they came round asking, going from door to door to ask if anyone had any room for anyone. They came to mum and she said she had the girls and she couldn't take anyone in – she was quite wary at first. Our neighbour said, 'That wee back bedroom, Jean could share with Maggie and Mary, you know you could let them have that room,', but mum said, 'It's a short bed,' for it was a smaller room and the bed had been shortened to fit in and at that time of course it was all right for me. This small Polish officer said, 'Could I come up and try?'[1] and he came up and lay down in front of the bed and it was all right for him. He came and stayed with us and remained a friend till after the war.

The first night the lieutenant (we always called him that though he was a major later) came to us, we were sitting in the living room and mum offered him the paper to read, and he took it, but afterwards when he got to know us he said he couldn't read a word. He couldn't speak English or read English. There were classes held up at Kingsland after school for the

---
[1] Presumably through an interpreter.

Polish soldiers to learn English and I used to have a wee book that I had since I was younger. There were pictures, like a picture of an apple and an A, and he would look at it and say 'apple' and look at the picture, and then I would cover up the picture and he would read the word. Then I'd cover up the word and he'd look at the picture and say 'apple'. He often said he learnt more from that than he did from the class. My war work – teaching someone English!

VJ Day, that was the victory in Japan, was on 15 August and that was my twelfth birthday and there was a bonfire that night. It was up on the old golf course, on Morning Hill, going up Edderston Road and across on the right before you come to Cademuir.

Colonel Aidan Sprot was occupied with distinguished war service abroad until retirement in 1962. At home, Peebles was defended by the Home Guard, whose protection of Peebles is still evident in the landscape, as he describes:
There are a lot of remains of defence work in the parish from the '39 -'45 War.[2] They include a lot of Home Guard defence things that were made. We have the remains of the Home Guard Rifle Range where they practised shooting up Glensax. Up at the back here at Crookston are the remains of three or four sangas in the scree. Sanga is an Urdu name for a – well, it's meant to be similar to a slit trench to protect you from enemy fire, but on rocky places you've got to pile up rocks in front of you because you can't dig down. It's supposed to give you the same protection and there are several of them from which you get a very good view of our little road coming out from Peebles to Cademuir which I suppose any enemy who got their tanks this far, if bridges were blown and they had to remain this side of the river, would use to come round this way. Also there are one or two brick small sheds, huts, which I think were ammunition stores for the Home Guard.

Willie Euman and his brothers all served in the war. They longed to celebrate their return with a walk on the hills, and this is what happened next!
Sandy was in the Navy. I was RAF and our older brother, Rob, was the Royal Scots. Rob saw the whole war – he was in the Territorials before the war and he was mobilised the day before war was declared. So Rob would be six and a half years away. My brothers and I between us had fifteen years in what they call World War Two; fifteen years!

---
[2] These have been investigated and collated by Ian Brown of Peebles.

Always one for the great outdoors, I'm pleading to roam and watching with interest the concerned groupings in their latest endeavour to bring out new legislation, pleading to roam after our fifteen years in the Services. We used to mention in our correspondence the great day that would come again when we were back and would take to the hills and all the rest of it. This happened, here we were demobbed and back, in civvies, in mufti again, so we arranged a walk.   Not a marathon. We would go out along the Glasgow Road to the end of the Neidpath woods and we would take to the hills and work our way over Hamilton Hill, which is very dear to most people in Peebles. When we got about half a mile into the hills, we met a character with a naked firearm, a shotgun, who we learned later, although we had a strong suspicion, was what we call a gamekeeper. And this is how, on our long looked-for return to the hills and the great outdoors, we were accosted by this character. 'Do you know you're trespassing?'

We had just ensured that this man would have a free existence by lending in a small way our efforts to defeat the tyrant Adolf Hitler and his quest for world domination and this, it would seem, this guy or his employers never took on board at all.   'Do you know you're trespassing?'….. that fellow never came nearer to death! At that moment in time, he never came nearer to instant extinction. He'll never know that. I just thought, 'If ever murder was justified!'   In this particular situation, our long-awaited jaunt into the hills to enjoy the great outdoors again, here was this character with the gun, 'Do you know you're trespassing?'

Chapter 8
TOURISM AND TRANSPORT

Peebles has always attracted visitors, even before the time of universal travel by private car. Visitors came by bus, and until 1963 there were the trains.

Pam Fairless tells of the way visitors were made welcome before the war:
A lot of people came and stayed for holidays. There were landladies in the town at that time. There was a lady who stayed near us, Granny Oliver they called her, and she always had lodgers. They came from Glasgow or wherever and she would let out a bedroom and a sitting room and provide all the food. That was how they did it. It wasn't Bed and Breakfast, they got their meals provided as well.

In fact my grandmother kept lodgers sometimes here. They came in the summertime. They came as lodgers but finished up being friends and they used to come every year. I suppose they lived with the family, almost.

There were hotels, of course, and the Hydro was there. Then they had the Scottish Tennis Championships at the Hydro. On the banking that goes down to the tennis court, they made tiers and they put planking where people sat and watched the championships.

They also had all their special baths there with it being a spa. The people came for that as well. The people didn't come in cars but by train. There was a little bus, the Hydro bus, that was always at the station with this man in uniform who met them and took their luggage and took them up to the Hydro in this little bus. It had its door at the back. It wasn't very posh, actually it was a bit tinny looking. Those were the days when you went up to afternoon tea for half a crown and had the orchestra playing. Local people sometimes went up for a treat.

Jean Thomson remembers summer visitors as well as a holiday for her own family which began with a disaster:
The first year we were in George Street, mum took in summer visitors. They used to bring their food in. I can remember one family – they brought their food in and mum would cook it for them, and they would come back at lunchtime and have their food. I suppose they had their tea as well if they stayed the night.

And we went on holiday too - my cousins Margaret and Mary, and mum and dad and me. Mum and dad and myself had gone to Portobello one Sunday to have a look for rooms for our holiday and we were in this house and mum and dad decided they'd take those two rooms and we'd go there for our week's holiday. So that's what we did. And mum had the idea of packing all our clothes in a big trunk that my dad had brought home when he'd come home from Africa just after the Second World War. All our clothes were put into it for the five of us and it was going to save us carrying anything. It was to be sent by train and would arrive at Portobello and be delivered to the house. Now mum had packed away a bottle of Syrup of Figs, which during the journey broke. I don't know what else was spoilt but I know that my nice new straw hat was ruined! I don't think too many things were ruined but everything was sticky and had to be washed.

Mother got the food in and the landlady cooked it. There was a big round table in one of the rooms and when the lady came in to serve the meal, she used to have strings – I don't know how many strings of beads round her head and a great big hat on. Margaret and Mary couldn't stop laughing. Mum always sat them with their back to the door and she would try to keep the lady engaged in conversation so she couldn't see them laughing. That lady was a good cook, the food she gave us was good, even though she was all dressed up to the nines to serve the meal!

Peggy Ferguson and Mary Johnstone have long ago memories of gentle forms of transport:
Mary: You used to see horses, not cars. I mind the wee sprinter, the high stepper, that used to come up from Kailzie. You know, it was one of these lovely ponies and a wee trap, aye. Then of course the Hydro had a carriage that went down to the station for the guests.
Peggy: Ellersey, at that day, they had a horse-drawn carriage for holiday folk. It took quite a lot of people, it must have taken about twenty people maybe, and Mr Thompson brought a wee ladder for them to get into it, and I think there'd be four horses. It would take the people just round Peebles.

There weren't a lot of hotels, no. There were lots of people just came down and booked a room – like in our holidays, your mother booked a room.

Leonard Grandison remembers day-trippers....
Peebles attracted people for holidays to an extent, but I think it was the short breaks – Edinburgh Holiday or Spring Holiday or something like that. Queues, particularly for the buses – massive queues for the Edinburgh bus.

The stop was where it still is today and the queues were right along past the Chambers Institute. Peebles has obviously been a favourite place for people to go for a day out. If you read Anna Buchan's books, she writes about people coming for holidays – she was still writing when I was a lad.

...and passes on a memory told him by his father:
My father told me he got a holiday from school to see the first cars going through Peebles, which must have been about 1904 or '05. I suspect it wasn't just any old car going through but that it was one of the reliability trials that were a feature of motoring in those days, you know, when they went from London to Edinburgh or Torquay or something like that. I don't know anything more about it, but he always used to go on about getting the holiday. To live from that to seeing men go on the moon – quite incredible!

As we know from the minutes of the Tweeddale Society, members went on day trips by charabanc to many places of interest in the Borders and other parts of Scotland.

Fig. 18   Charabanc in Berwick-on-Tweed with Tweeddale Society members aboard, 21 May 1930.

Willie and Sandy Euman look back to the golden age of transport:
Sandy: We saw the demise of the horse, the horse and cart. The horses working on the farms disappeared – got a huge push in the wartime when they introduced the Fordson tractor on some of the farms. This was the beginning of the end for the horses on the farms.

Transport began to be dominated by the railway. In our young days, they had just started the bus service to Edinburgh, in the late twenties. And we had the train as a means of travel before. A lot of people working in the mill at Innerleithen or vice versa travelled by train.

Willie: I could begin this little story by saying we were happier in the life when we were young – it was a gentler age, everything was nicer, quieter, it was a beautiful existence. I come back to the railways. It may interest a lot of people to know that the Galashiels-Peebles branch line was the last to be installed in Scotland. We were ten years later than any other railway laid out in Scotland simply because a farmer and landowner was opposed to it. He was a landowner beyond Walkerburn and he said no and that was the end of it. It was to be another ten years after most people enjoyed railway links, another ten years before we got a railway line from Galashiels to Peebles.

Audrey Edwards and Ilene Brown remember the traffic on the streets of Peebles:
The Hamiltons had a horse and cart which was known as the Chip Cart. It came along Dean Park and stood in the Northgate (at the Couchee Righ) selling chips cooked on the cart! There was also the Rag and Bone man who pushed his cart through the town. Very obvious with balloons tied to the cart and blowing in the wind. Fish Ladies with fresh fish for sale were a frequent sight. The Co-op Bakery horse and cart came every Saturday.

Fig. 19   George Jack (Jinglin' Geordie) with 'Soor Dook' Milk Cart outside The Greentree Hotel, Eastgate.

Kinnaird Cunningham tells of his grandparents' visits to Manor Valley and the advantages of travelling by train:
My grandparents lived over near Dunbar and when they decided to come over here, which was usually twice a year, once in the early summer and once for shooting grouse, they would pack everything up and they'd stop the main line train from London to Edinburgh at a little place called Belton. They would put everything on the train and I think they probably had a coach to themselves, knowing them. The coach was detached at Waverley and then they would change the coach on to the line that came down to Peebles. Then they went round the little loop that took you round to the Caledonian Railway Station which came out this way. They would stop at the bottom of the valley at Lyne Station and the wagonette would have gone ahead and would come down and meet them off the train. They would have dinner off the same cutlery as they had at breakfast at the other side of the country! So things were kind of different in those days, but that just happened twice a year when they came over.

We were very sorry to see the railway go. My father used to go into Edinburgh every day on the train. That was so regular that the station master would hold the train up, 'Wait a moment. I see Mr Cunningham's car just coming in to park now.' I don't think we ever drove in to Edinburgh. We always went in on the train, occasionally on the bus, so we were quite sorry when that went in 1963. 'Pomathorn change for Penicuik,' I remember. I never discovered where Pomathorn was but it was one of the places the train stopped at, presumably not far from Penicuik.

The line from Lyne went to Carstairs where it was very cold and you had to stand around waiting for trains to come and go. That was where they divided the Edinburgh and Glasgow portions of the trains coming from the south. I used to come up on that from time to time too, otherwise it was the night sleeper from St. Pancras, get off at Galashiels and get met there if I was lucky.

Jean Thomson recalls stations and train journeys and remembers all the stations between Peebles and Edinburgh:
Now a thing I remember, both prewar, wartime and after the war, was Peebles Station. It used to be a great thrill standing on the platform waiting for the train, going into Edinburgh for the shops or maybe getting off at Portobello for the seaside, or going down to Gala to visit my aunt. At the station, there were flower beds dug out opposite where the actual station was, so if you look at the banking on the new relief road and see the big long flowerbeds, they were directly opposite the platform. There was one stationmaster who was really keen on the gardens and he planted them out and they were always nice and they're still there. That station was the LNER.[1]

Then the LMS[2] of course was over at Dukehaugh direction. In fact I think Tweedbridge Court is maybe more or less on the site of the station there.[3]

At Gala we used often to get a wee train that ran on the branch line to Selkirk. It didn't seem to be a steam engine, it just seemed to be a carriage, and it was called 'the coffee pot' – that was its nickname – and it went along the six miles to Selkirk.

The stations' names are lovely going into Edinburgh. You left Peebles and then it was Eddleston, Leadburn, Pomathorn for Penicuik, Roslin Lea, Roslin, Hawthorndean, Eskbank for Dalkeith, Portobello, and then from there sometimes it stopped at Millerhill and sometimes you bypassed that station and went straight to Edinburgh – it depended on which way the train went.[4]

Sheila Murray, Arthur Crittell and Aidan Sprot all give the facts about stations and railway lines in Peebles, each giving details which add up to a full picture.
Sheila Murray:
There were two railway stations. One was at the end of Station Road with trains going between Edinburgh and the Borders. The main road out of the town to Edinburgh now passes along where the station was and the railway yard is now the carpark. The second railway line started at the station which is now Dukehaugh and took passengers to Glasgow, passing through what we called the 'Halfmile Tunnel' and over the Tweed by the Viaduct Bridge. Many of the up-country pupils came by this train to Peebles High School.

Arthur Crittell was ten years old when the last railway train ran from Peebles to Edinburgh. He remembers being taken on the train:
There were two stations and I remember going to Edinburgh on the train from the station in Dean Park with my mother and father. In 1963, it ceased to be under Beeching. They closed on the Sunday night and took up the rails on the Monday morning. And when they closed the station, they altered the Edinburgh Road to run along where the railway line had been and did away with what we called the Sand Bridge up over Dean Park, where the road used to go.
The line from the other station which led to Glasgow through Broughton was closed in 1954. The station was still there for a bit but it was all pulled down when they built Tweedbridge Court.

---
[1] London and North Eastern Railway. The only relic of the station buildings is the coal office in Edinburgh Road carpark.
[2] London Midland and Scottish.
[3] The railway arch is still there, under the road south of Tweed Bridge.
[4] See Anon (probably Chambers), Peebles and its neighbourhood, with a run on Peebles Railway, Edinburgh, 1856.

And Aidan Sprot:
I suppose everyone knows – maybe new arrivals don't in fact know – that there were two railway stations, one to Glasgow, one to Edinburgh, with a link in between. The link crossing the river was just downstream from the footbridge – you can see the embankment. The new by-pass road, as we call it, from Edinburgh to Gala, past the carpark, that was more or less the line of the railway, and then you were turned off and went under the road by the Tweeddale Garage and you can see the embankment and there's an extraordinary house. Instead of being square, it's at an angle, and that was because the railway went there. People say, 'Oh, Peebles doesn't have a railway,' but they had two stations – incredible!

Leonard Grandison has more stories to tell of trains and buses:
Now 1940 – there was certainly a strong story at that time that the King and Queen at that time spent a night in the tunnel.[5] I've always believed it was true and then somebody not all that many years ago said it wasn't. Maybe they were visiting Clydebank or some place like that. It was a single track going through the tunnel, on the line from Peebles to Biggar, and you then went either to Carstairs or Symington, sometimes you changed trains and sometimes you just went straight through.

1942-ish they were running the buses on the Edinburgh-Galashiels service with gas generators on the back of them. They were like a big sort of boiler with coke in them and this was because petrol was short. I spoke to someone about it who knew what I was talking about and he thought that, because the route to Peebles was pretty hilly, the engines running on this gas were not as efficient as they would be on a flat area. I think they took them to use in East Lothian where they would run better.

At the Caley station, you know, the one down at Dukehaugh, there was a railway turntable. Some of the bigger kids, we all used to go down and help to push the engines round. Strictly speaking it wasn't the end of the line because it went round and connected up with the North British Railway on the other station. It went across the Tweed and round there but that was only used once in a blue moon. I mean, the two companies were not exactly on best terms.

---

[5] Halfmile Tunnel on the former Caledonian Railway, later London Midland and Scottish, as described by Sheila Murray. They sleps in the comfort of the Royal Train.

When we first built our offices above the yard, which must have been in the late '50s, we could see the trains going from Gala to Edinburgh. We never thought they would stop. As a boy I used to spend hours watching them shunting. Now we all have cars. I never used the train to go to Edinburgh because I couldn't get home. It was absolutely ridiculous, it never ceased to make me mad. You could get to Edinburgh fine, but unless it was a Saturday night, the last train left Edinburgh about 8 o'clock. I mean it was run for the benefit of the railway men not for the customers, and it made me absolutely mad. The train took about the same time as the bus because it went away round by Millerhill, it went in a great big circle, but it was far more comfortable in the winter, and if you wanted to read something, it was far better than going about in the bus.

⁶As described by Aidan Sprot. The North British Railway became part of the London and North Eastern Railway.

Chapter 9

GROWTH AND CHANGE

The constant themes of all our contributors are the changes that have come about in Peebles during their lifetimes – changes at work and at leisure, in travel, at school, in health care – indeed in almost every aspect of daily life. Our purpose in collecting their memories has been to record these changes and to preserve eye-witness evidence of how Peebles was before they took place.   Some aspects of Peebles have stayed the same but the changes have made a bigger impression on Peebleans.

The changes and the growth have taken place hand in hand.   The rapid social and economic developments of the late twentieth century affected every aspect of our lives and we cannot go back.   But we can look back and remember to conserve for the new generation the memories of how things used to be.

In common with many towns, the most visible changes have taken place in the High Street.   Many of our contributors remember in great detail the shops that used to be in the Old Town and the High Street and how different shopping used to be.   Sometimes their memories overlap and each detail adds depth to the picture of life in Peebles as it was within living memory.

James Renwick's father had a grocery business in the Old Town:
I was born in Peebles, in Tweed Avenue down by the bowling green near the Gytes.   My grandfather was a shepherd up Manor, but during the hard times my father moved to Leith.   In 1900, my father returned from Leith and took up the shop in the bottom of the Old Town, the grocer's shop – J.L. Renwick and Sons.   That was where the 'Out and About' place is now. And I moved it over the road – it's the Co-op nowadays, it used to be Alldays, next to the Castle Warehouse.   I converted that into a supermarket and was there until I sold out to Karen Campbell twenty years ago.   And I had a shop in Innerleithen too, where the TAVO charity shop is now.

The shops all made a good living in those days but the supermarkets killed them all off.   You can't compete with them, you see, simply can't compete.   There used to be half a dozen grocers' shops in the High Street, four chemists, at least half a dozen sweetie shops, two tobacconists, another ironmonger, fish shops.   And customers were loyal.   If you went to our shop, you wouldn't go anywhere else.   You prided yourself that you got everything that your customers asked for, even if you had to go to another shop and buy it. And in the old days we used to go round and collect orders at the houses and we had country vans too, going round the country. We had two country vans, and the message boys went round two or three mornings to various houses, picked up the orders, made them up and delivered them. In those days the housewife never needed to go out of the house because she had rolls delivered in the morning, she had milk delivered to her, she had the butchers' and the grocers' boys calling at the house, so she didn't really need to go out.

Getting message boys was never a problem. Boys don't do that sort of thing now. You can hardly get boys to deliver newspapers. There was nothing else for them then in Peebles, just the shops or the mills, that was all there was. There was no commuting to Edinburgh.

We were a very much more close-knit community. Wednesday was a half day, everybody closed on a Wednesday, so there were various activities, football and so forth, on a Wednesday, and on Sunday, of course, the place was closed down – there was nothing open on a Sunday. That made for a very much closer-knit community than it is today.

Ken McOwan lived over his father's shop in the High Street and he remembers almost every shop and shopkeeper in the Old Town and the High Street from the 1920s and 1930s. We'll start with a selection in the Old Town:
At the top of the Old Town, I remember there was a tailor, Skelton his name was and he was where the Red Cross charity shop is now. He used to go about very correctly dressed, with his frock coat and his tight trousers and he used to have a little moustache. The next one down was the fishmongers, and of course there was Harben the fruiterers next door – Harben the fruiterer, he was a councillor. The next one down was Castle Warehouse as it is now – that used to be Anderson, drapers. He was provost for a while in the town when I was very young. Then coming down the hill, you get to a garage, a cycle shop, where the Co-op is now. If you went round the back, the cycles were up the top part by Greenside and in a garage they used to do car maintenance.

And then of course round the corner was the huge Co-op. You remember that, do you? The old wifies used to settle down on a form there with their pass books and they used to call out your number, and they went up to the counter and were served and got their dividend, every quarter I think it was. That was a great day, the divvy day. Then the cheque office next door, I remember that as well. It was a sort of glassed-off bit with little cubby holes where you brought your store checks and you could buy goods and your groceries. Then across the road there was the Store as well – the drapers as far as I remember.   But it's funny how changes come about. They're all different now but I can still remember them all. There's quite a few businesses gone to the wall since the advent of the supermarkets.

From Ken's tour of the shops in the High Street, we have picked out some highlights:
At Bank House, that was the Buchan's house. Anna Buchan who was O. Douglas (you know about her books) and her brother Wattie Buchan who was town clerk lived there. And next to them was the Commercial Bank of Scotland, now the Royal Bank which has moved along. After they moved, that became a fruiterers, but they packed up after a while. Next door to that was the ice cream place. And next to that was a china shop. Nothing but china and if you wanted any cups, saucers, whatever, they had it.   I remember there were great big shelves all round with all sorts of china pieces.   It was quite a busy little shop, as far as I remember.   Next door was Crichton the butchers and next door to that, Easton's the stationers. I remember Mr Easton, a very tall man who was Superintendent of the Sunday School at St. Andrew's Church.......

Next to the Crown Hotel was a chemist, Douglas the chemist. He was a little thin-faced man with clipped specs on his nose. And there were rows and rows of coloured bottles along the shelves, the pharmacy bottles with Latin names on them – a nice little shop.   And next door to that was The Buttercup, the dairy. My mother used to send me along the street to get a pound of butter and there was a great big wadge of butter on a china stand. They used to cut a piece off with these little paddles and pat it into a block and measure and weigh it and then wrap it up and there you were.   There was always a queue in that place.   I remember over the door where you went in it had a beautiful tile picture of a milkmaid all done in coloured tiles.   It was quite a work of art – green and yellow, green fields and a cow there and a milkmaid – it was wonderful.

Then of course you've got Scott Brothers, the original Scott brothers. They used to walk up and down on the bare boards of the shop and they both had great big tacketty boots on.   There was Willie Scott, and then the sons have come on and the grandsons after them and I think the great-grandsons are in there now......

Cowans the butchers, I remember going in there. You chose your meat and there was a glassed-in pay desk where you bought it.   There was always a woman sitting in there and that's where you'd pay, same as you have in Forsyth's today.

Fig. 20 Ken McOwan's father standing in the doorway of his shop in the High Street in the 1920s.

And then we come to our premises, which my father bought from somebody called Hislop, a watchmaker. After my father was demobbed at the end of the First World War, he came to Peebles and married my mother and started a jeweller's business then. The shop looked quite a bit different to what it is now, because it had two little windows each about two and a half feet wide and there was a little arch over the top of each window, and a middle arch was the door into the business and that was all given a new shop front in the late 1920s which is more or less as it is today. My father used to do optical business as well and there was sight-testing for buying glasses. We lived above the shop, of course, two storeys there, and next door, on the other side of the close, was Johnson the baker. They lived above the shop too and my mother and Mrs Johnson didn't get on too well. There was a dispute over the drying green at the back and they never spoke for years after that. They had two sons, Bob and David. David went away to South Africa and Bob took over when his father retired. They had the bakehouse at the back. Oh, I used to go in that bakehouse – I was quite fascinated with the ovens and all the bakers there covered in flour. And the confectioner, it was Bob at the time when his father was on the go. I used to watch him with his little bags of icing-sugar – he just squeezed all the icing-sugar out and decorated things with it like bride's cakes – it was quite fascinating to watch. It was quite a big bakehouse they had down the back there.[1] Then Medical Hall – that's changed very little, and then a grocers next door to that which was originally Percy Daniels and then Pym

---
[1] Now 'The Ovendoor Tea Room'.

Fig. 21 The shop after modernisation. Johnstone's the bakers and The Medical Hall to the right.

Scott. I can remember when we used to go along there for groceries when we lived in the High Street. Lady Hay of Haystoun, she used to come down to order her groceries in a chauffeur-driven car. Eventually that shop became the first supermarket in Peebles – Coopers that was. And now it's the bottle shop.

We've missed out the Benigno's. You know where the electrical shop is now? That was the Benigno's little shop – they were Italians. You used to go down a step into it and they used to make and sell all the ice cream in there. Their other shop was just past Coopers. It was a big shop, big stained glass window in the back a very big coffee-making machine all gleaming on the marble counter which used to make a noise like an express train. Benigno himself used to stand at the door of that place and he employed all his family as his assistants in the shops – two sons and about four daughters. He never appeared to do any work but he used to have a lot of trophies for shooting. Now he came to a bad end. I heard that he was deported in wartime as an enemy alien. A lot were sent away to the Isle of Man, but quite a lot were sent to Canada and a lot of them were lost, mainly Italians, when their ship was torpedoed. Johnnie, the eldest son took over the business. Benigno's ice cream was famous. It had a secret recipe which nobody knew but the old man and he handed over this recipe to Johnnie and Johnnie carried on and the ice cream was unique – nobody knew how to make it like that.

Ken describes some of the shops he could see from his bedroom window on the opposite side of the High Street.
There was the South of Scotland Electricity Board, and above that was a photographers, McNaught was the name. Next door to that was the corner shop which was originally a dairy, Dobson's. I can remember it quite clearly because we lived just across the road and I used to go across as a boy to get milk. It was always quite cool in that shop. They had a marble top and at the far end of the counter a great big white china bowl, it must have been a yard across in diameter and deep, and it was full of milk. They had a metal scoop with a hooked handle they hooked over the edge of the bowl which was a pint measure. They dipped it in and poured the milk into your jug and away you went. They lived above the shop too, and I used to play with the boy. At the back there they had a stairway that had a blue and red stained-glass window - I think it's still there.

Next door was Wetherston the saddlers. They specialised in riding kit and all leather goods. I remember the lovely smell of leather when you went in there – you know the sort of smell – and they had a workshop at the back where they used to do all sorts of work. I can see him now – a little fellow with a black apron. And then there was the Band Hall. The Peebles Silver Band, I daresay they still practise there. I used to lie in bed before going to sleep and hear the band practising over the road there and it used to lull me to sleep.

Fig. 22   The Fire Station as Ken saw it.

Ken could watch the comings and goings at the Fire Station from his window:
Then the Fire Station, oh, there was great excitement whenever there was a fire. I can remember when the fire engine was like a cart, four wheels all painted red and a big polished chimney thing. They had a fire going, I think it was coal fired, and they pulled it behind a horse. Later on, a lorry. This was probably to generate steam for the pump.

I can remember seeing this thing trundle along the street – I must have been very small at the time – with smoke coming out of the chimney at the top and polished brass all gleaming, red painted. Of course, afterwards they got a proper fire engine, a motorised one. They always kept it in there and there was always quite a rush when the fire alarm went.. All the local fellows who were in the fire brigade used to dash over, open the doors and out would come the fire engine and tear down the street ringing its bell. We used to get a bird's eye view of all this when we lived across the road.[2]

And next door to that was a grocers, Huish the grocers they called it, and they left the business to Nellie Nelson who was their assistant. Nellie was my mother's friend and lived above Scott Brothers.

Though Arthur Crittell's childhood memories are more recent, from the 1950s and 60s, Peebles has changed from the little town that he remembers from his young days:
It was a lot smaller than it is today. A lot more shops in the High Street – good quality shops. There were three butchers in the High Street and six or seven, possibly eight, grocers' shops, two wine merchants and no shops open after five o'clock selling alcohol. You had to go to a pub to buy your alcohol and they charged a levy.

Henry Liney's shop in the Old Town was a sweetie shop. He had what you would call a very first soda stream – a big glass bubble with water in it. You had the choice of a halfpenny drink or a penny drink. A penny drink was the equivalent of a pint of juice or pop and you got different flavours and at Christmas time he always had ginger ale on sale. Behind the counter was a big tray of all the penny things and at Christmas time he did a display of all the sweeties for Christmas.

At the top of March Street or Rosetta Road, where The Scent of Ginger is, was also a general stores run by Rob Stevenson. He was in the army in India and could do a lot of magic tricks, and at Christmas time he had a bag shop and he did a display as well of all the sweeties and different things you could buy at Christmas time. His biscuits were stored in tins in the shop. You could buy a quarter of biscuits of all different types – custard creams, bourbon biscuits, fig rolls, digestive biscuits, all loose.

---

[2] The Fire Service moved down to its present site on the old Caley station sidings, as Arthur Crittell reminded us.

The post office used to be in Northgate. I can just remember shops there, very vaguely, but when they demolished the shops, they found a big barrel of cider in the basement which Clyde the builders' men demolished in the afternoon and they were all rather tipsy when they came to have their photograph taken at the end of the afternoon. Jimmy Clyde said, 'I don't mind getting the photograph taken, but try not to smile too much!'

I worked for Skelton the tailors as a message boy when I was thirteen and he wore a morning suit and a bowler hat at his work. He had two daughters and a son who worked in the back shop making suits. I used to spend a lot of money up there. And up in the Old Town was the paper shop run by Miss Barber and up from that again there was a sweet shop and wool shop run by John Scott and his wife. When I was fourteen or fifteen, he had a barrow and I had to go up to the park in the summer to sell ice cream – push the barrow from the Old Town right away down to Hay Lodge Park to the swing to sell ice cream and then I had to push it back up the hill from the park to the shop.

The Co-op was the big thing in the town when I was small. The main part of the Coop was in the Old Town which was where the Castle Warehouse and the Forestry Commission is. They had a furniture shop, they had a ladies and gents outfitters, it had a cafe where Inglis the shoeshop is now, they had a barbers down the Northgate, they had a butchers' shop in Northgate where there's now flats, they had a butchers' shop up Elmbank, they had a bakers' shop where Snipp-It is now and at the back of there was what we called the Store – Court garages – and that was where the bakers was for the Co-op. And they had two travelling shops. Jimmy in the Old Town, he had a travelling shop on the road and it served the whole of Peeblesshire. Bill Neal, another Peebles man, had two travelling shops on the road in Peebles and he went round at night selling different wares. The Co-op had a butchers' van and two bakers' vans on the road. When I started school, they were drawn by horses which were kept in stables by the store.

There was a big bakers where the Royal Bank is now and they had a tearoom upstairs, very very popular. A pie was fourpence halfpenny – a pie is now 58 pence which is nearly 12 shillings in old money. The rolls are now 15 pence – three shillings in old money – my granny would turn in her grave!

The Royal Bank of Scotland was next to Buchan House. They moved to their present site when they altered Cuddy Bridge. Where accountants are next to the Tontine was the British Linen Bank. It was amalgamated with the Bank of Scotland which was always where it is now. Jim Arnold was the manager at the time. He had a very good manner as a bank manager and that's where they kept the silver for the church for the communion.

The High Street's changed dramatically in the last twenty-five years, not for the better, for the worse I think. The sort of change is remarkable because of the impact of the supermarkets. The shops that I knew have more or less disappeared and there are lots of charity shops now.

Sheila Laurie remembers the childhood joy of having a few pennies to spend in the shops in the Old Town:
A few of us would go to Henry Liney's sweet shop at the foot of the Old Town, where along the back wall was a bench set where we would dangle our legs after buying a halfpenny sasparilla drink from this machine that Henry worked – it made a swooshing noise.[3] After the drink, the other halfpenny had to be carefully spent choosing the best value sweeties. Mrs Liney would soon be shouting if she thought we were too long in the choosing. Other times there was Miss Renwick who had a wee shop opposite where we got broken biscuits and broken chocolate – no packaged stuff in those days.

Ilene Brown remembers the kindness of a neighbour:
I was brought up in the country, next to McGillivary's market garden at Eshiels. The fields were very busy at berry picking time, lots of young people earned their pocket money this way.[4]

McGillivary's large greengrocer and flower shop was in the High Street, now part of the Tourist Information Centre. Maggie McGillivary, the sister, ran the shop. She lived in Elcho Street, not at Eshiels. I remember the queues when word got out, 'McGillivary's have Canadian apples!' This would have been in the late forties. My sister and I were gifted our wedding bouquets from Mr McGillivary.

McGillivary's went on to have a good haulage company in the Northgate, on the site which was Plenderlieth and Stevenson's haulage company.

Isabel and Duncan Taylor are disturbed by the changes that they see in Peebles, but are pleased to remember one thing that stays the same:
Isabel: I spent twenty years down south. I came back home and that's when I noticed the awful difference. I couldn't believe what had happened. Nothing changes for the better, that's how it is. We love our town and I hope the people coming into it now, because there's a lot coming in, would just say what they came here for and use what we've got and don't try to change it and change us....

---

[3] This was the soda stream described by Arthur Crittell.
[4] See p33.

Duncan: There's no such thing in Scotland as trespass. You can go anywhere you like if you pay them some money – this goes back to old Scots law. If you go on someone's land, you hand them a silver coin of the realm and that covers you for damage and everything. People can walk through a garden and you can do nothing about it.

Isabel: And I hope nobody ever changes it because that's how it should be. People should be able to own their country. It doesn't belong to anybody, you know, it belongs to everybody. What you should do is to respect people's land. If you go for a walk, as long as you shut the gate and behave yourself, you should be able to walk freely. No farmer ever tried to keep us out, did they, Duncan?

Sheila Murray recognises what is happening to Peebles:
Peebles is very different today and many of us who remember the town as it once was regret changes that have taken place, but change is inevitable and must be accepted.[5]

Willie Euman reflects on the situation with more optimism, so he shall have the last word:
I passed some very happy years playing football with Peebles Rovers, and at that time it was quite common to get about a thousand people watching the Peebles Rovers and the population then was just about 5000 in Peebles, so it was very very much a footballing town.

    The town itself has changed too, from a little factory town – tweed mills – it's now more residential. So it's no longer the same Peebles that we knew. However, we don't want to be parochial about this. We should welcome all the newcomers to Peebles. I was an incomer myself, seventy-two years ago.[6] So I often think things come in a circle from five hundred years when Peebles was a wee hamlet and somebody wanted to come in and build a house and they said, 'Oh horror of horrors, we don't want any more people in here.' We would never have had Peebles.

    So let's welcome people in. It's simply realising it's changed, the composition of the town, from the time of mill workers, textile workers, to a town with many people either living here and travelling to Edinburgh or retired here on independent means.

---

[5] In 2005, a survey by the New Economic Forum praised the unique character of Peebles which was found to be one of the most diverse shopping towns in Britain. Bob Corsie, joint chairman of the Peebles Retail Association, said it was a triumph for the traders and the town; 'The new retailers have recognised the heritage of the High Street, and so the unique appeal that Peebles has for local and visiting shoppers has been preserved.'
Peeblesshire News, 10 June 2005.
[6] From Innerleithen, six miles away.

SOME USEFUL AND INTERESTING BOOKS

- Old Peebles   Rhona Wilson   Stenlake Publishing, 1998.
- Glimpses of Old Peebles from the collection of R. B. Robb and E. R. Stevenson   Royal Burgh of Peebles Callants' Club, reprinted 1990.
- Peebles and its People   Royal Burgh of Peebles Callant's Club, 2003.
- History of Peebles 1850-1990   J. L. Brown and I C. Lawson   Mainstream Publishing, 1979.
- Peebles March Riding and Beltane Queen Festival Centenary Book, 1899-1999. Research compiled and edited by Douglas Wright. Peebles March Riding and Beltane Festival Queen Committee, 1999.
- Peebles Guildry Corporation   anon   Peebles, 2004
- Peebles Railways   Peter Marshall   Oakwood Press, 2005.
- The Last Trains, (1) Edinburgh and S. E. Scotland   Moorfoot Publishing, 1990.
- Peebles 1906   Old Ordnance Survey Maps, Godfrey Edition, 1996.
- 100 Years of Kingsland, Life in a Primary School 1901-2001 Compiled and edited by Alistair Macpherson   Kingsland Centenary Association, 2003.
- Tweed Rivers   New writing and art inspired by the rivers of the Tweed catchment. Edited by Ken Cockburn and James Carter   Luath Press Ltd, 2005.
- The Source of Manor   Lyne and Manor Youth Group, 1998.
- Leaves from the Life of a Country Doctor   Clement Bryce Gunn Foreword by John Buchan   First published, 1935, reprinted Birlinn, 2002.
- "O. Douglas". The Story of Anna Buchan   Sheila Scott   31 High Street Biggar, 1993.

INDEX

Anderson, drapers, 115
angling, 8-9
apples, 34, 122
apprenticeship, 56
Arnold, J., Manager of Bank of Scotland, 122
Auction Mart, 35
auctioneer, 36, 57

bagpipes, 70
bailer, 46
bailiff, 7, 9-11
Baden-Powell, Agnes, 87-8
Ballantyne's Mill, 20, 52
Band Hall, 119
Band of Hope, 73-4
Bank House, 83, 116
banks, 91, 116, 121
Barber, Miss, shopkeeper, 121
barley, 42-3
Barns House, 81
Barton, Miss, teacher, 27
Beltane, 74-80, 82, 89
Benigno's ice cream, 118
Bible classes, 72, 74
Biggar, 43, 92, 112
Biggiesknowe, 8
Black, Albert, Elder, 85
Blackface sheep, 40, 43
blacksmiths, 38, 49
Blackwell, Charles, headmaster of Kingsland School, 28
boat hole, 9, 58, 66
Bonnington Farm, 40, 43-9
Bonong, Miss, teacher, 27
Border Leicester sheep, 40
Borders General Hospital, 87
Borthwick, Nellie, 88
Boston Cream, 29, 31
Boyd, Robert, First Courtier 1949, 75
Boys' Brigade, 89
Briggett, Bridgegate, 69
British Linen Bank, 91, 121
Broughton, 35, 61, 64, 87, 112
Bruce, Johnny, blacksmith, 38
Buchan, Anna, 72, 82-3, 108, 116
       John, 1st Lord Tweedsmuir, 82-3
       Walter, 82-3, 116
Burgh Hall, 69, 76, 87
Burnett, Misses, shopkeepers, 22
Burns, Robert, 57-8
buses, 15, 46, 102, 106-7, 109, 112-3
Buttercup dairy, 56, 116

Cademuir, 10, 56, 104
Cairns family, 37
Caledonian Road, 35
Caledonian station, 110, 120n
Cardrona, 14

carriers, 18
cars, 15, 46, 108
carts, 18, 109
Castle Warehouse, 57, 115, 121
cattle, 36-8, 40-2, 47
cattle grids, 95-7
cattle market, 42, 54
Cauld, 7, 9, 58, 87
Chambers Institute, 69, 100, 108
charabanc, 71, 108
Cheviot sheep, 40
Christmas, 11, 21, 49, 60, 63, 72-4, 82-3, 120
churches, 72-4, 83-6, 89
cinemas, 68-9, 72
Clare, Miss, teacher, 28
Clark Place, 35-6, 41, 54
cloth, 55
clothes, 21-3, 25, 102
Clyde, Jimmy, builders, 121
Clydebank, 98, 112
Clydesdale horses, 38-9
coal, 15, 21, 62
collie dogs, 35-6
Coltman, Mrs, 43
combine harvester, 42, 46, 50
concerts, 72, 79
Connor Street, 14
Coronation Street, 65
Co-op, 109, 114-5, 121
copperplate writing, 25
Cowan, butchers, 116
crime, 91-3
Crichton, Bill, actor, 72
Crichton, butchers, 116
Crookston, 40, 104
Cross Kirk, 29, 77
Cross Street, 35
Crown Hotel, 116
Crowning Ladies, 75-7
Cruikshank, Ian, organist, 84
Cuddy, 8, 12-4, 24, 58-9
Cuddy Brae Lane, 14
Cuddy Bridge, 83n, 98, 121
Cuddyside, 13, 23-4
Cumming, Mrs, 83
Cummings, Alistair, 88
curling pond, 14, 69, 87
curling tongs, 20-3
cycling, 15, 68

Dalatho, 102
dairies, 38, 47, 56, 116, 119
dairy farms, 38, 40, 47-9
Damcroft, 13, 53-4
Damcroft Mill, 13
Damdale, 13, 62
Damdale Mill, 53-4
dams, 7-8
dancing, 68-70, 74, 76
Davies, Walter, chemist, 63

125

Dean Park, 18, 109, 111
Denison, Walter, 89
Dobson's dairy, 119
Douglas, O., see Anna Buchan
Douglas, chemist, 116
Dovecot, 13, 103
dressmaking, 22, 56
Drill Hall, 69, 74, 76, 99, 100
drying greens, 24
dye house, 54
dykes, 16, 43

East Brae, 14
Eastgate, 20
Easton, stationers, 116
Edderston Farm, 37-8
Edderston Road, 14, 41, 104
Eddleston, 102, 111
Edinburgh, 7, 16, 46, 49, 60, 69, 90-2
          98, 101-5, 109-13
Edston, 37
Elcho Street, 20, 122
Elcho Street Brae, 35
electricity, 44-5
Eliots Park, 18, 22, 26, 36-7, 68, 78
Eliots Park Farm, 36
Elmbank, 121
Empire Cinema, 60, 69
Erskine, Lady, 87-8
   Veronica, 87-8
Eshiels, 33, 49, 122
evacuees, 98, 101
exciseman, 57-8
excursions, 71, 108

farming, farms, 35-50, 64, 108
Ferguson, Sam, Boys' Brigade, 89
fertiliser, 41, 45, 50
fire, 53-4, 60
Fire Station, 119-120
First World War, 18, 31, 62, 65, 88, 116
fishing, 8-11
flooding, 7, 12-4
football, 70, 123
Forby, Miss, teacher, 27
forests, forestry, 40, 50-1, 56
Forsyth's, baker and butcher, 85, 116
funerals, 84
Fyfe, Alexander, bank manager and lawyer, 91
   Gordon, 93

Galashiels, 109-113
gales, 14, 17
Galloway cattle, 41
gas, 62
George Street, 20, 103, 106
Geralds, Miss, teacher, 27
Gibson Place, 69
Gilchrist, Willie, 38

Girls Guides, 77, 87-9
Glasgow, 66-7, 110-2
Glenormiston, 53
Glensax, 40-1, 104
Gordon, Harry, entertainer, 101
Graham Street, 30
Graham, Willie, watchmaker, 61
Grandison's Plasterers, 58-60
Grant, Kenneth, 84
gravel, 58-60
Greenside, 21, 23, 62, 66, 79, 81
Greenside Laundry, 23
Guildry Corporation of Peebles, 85-6
Gunn, Dr. Clement, 19, 63-4, 81-3
gutterbluid, 18, 89
Gypsy Glen, 68

Haig, Earl, 67, 81
Halyrude School, 27-8, 30
Hamilton, Rev. James, Minister of Old
   Parish Church, 84
Hamilton Hill, 26n, 27, 105
Hammond, Alec, 89
Harben, fruiterers, 115
Harper, Miss, teacher, 28
harvest, 42, 45
Hay, Sir Duncan, 40n, 43
   Lady, 77, 117
Hay Lodge, 34, 99
Hay Lodge Health Centre, 63, 65
Hay Lodge Park, 30, 79, 121
Haystoun, 40, 43, 45
haymaking, 49
Hearn, Miss, teacher, 28
hedgehogs, 95-7
Highland Show, 47-8
High School, 25-8, 61, 70, 78, 111
High Street, 60, 69, 72, 79, 83, 91, 114-123
High Tig, 26
Highers, 25-6, 61
Highland cattle, 41
Hislop, Charlie, 9
Hislop, watchmakers, 116-7
holidays, 62, 68, 72, 107
Home Guard, 104
Horsburgh Castle, 14, 30
horses, 18, 38-9, 42-3, 45, 78, 107-8, 121
Hundleshope, 27, 40, 43
Hydro, 30, 60-2, 69, 76-7, 85-8, 99-101, 103,
               106

ice cream, 70, 118, 121
Innerleithen, 20, 61, 87, 99, 109, 114
Innerleithen Pipe Band, 70

Jack, Miss, teacher, 28
Jack family, 37-8, 74-6
Jinglin' Geordie, 37, 109
Johnson's, bakers, 117-8
Johnston, Miss, teacher, 27

Kailzie, 107
Kerfield Farm, 12
Kerr, Jean, 61
King George VI, 53
Kingsland School, 25-8, 78-9, 90, 103
Kingsmeadows House, 11-2, 66
Kingsmeadows Road, 14
Kirkland Street, 22

Lanark, 46
Land Army, Women's, 44
landladies, 106-7
lawyers, 83, 90-5
Laverick, Edward, Town Clerk of Peebles, 93
Lea Lodge, 7
Leadburn, 14, 64, 98, 111
Leckie Church, 72, 89
legal practice, 90-5
Lindores, 64, 66, 81
Liney, Henry, sweetie shop, 120,122
lodgers, 106
Logie, Miss, teacher, 27
Lord Lieutenant of Tweeddale, 43, 86-7, 93
Lowe Donalds, 52, 55
luckpenny, 42
Lyon, John, 69

McCartney, Crear, 85
McFarlane, Miss, teacher, 29
MacGillivary's, strawberry farm and greengrocer, 33, 122
Mackie, John, County Clerk, 91
Mackintosh, Rennie, 18
McNaught, photographer, 119
mangle, 21, 23
Manor Valley, 10-1, 15, 29, 42-3, 46, 56, 64
Manor Valley Sanatorium, 81
Manson, Dr., 66
March Street, 19, 22-3, 30, 41, 52, 72-3, 79, 120
Martin, Dr., 66
markets, 35-7, 41-2, 46
Medical Hall, The, chemists, 63, 117-8
Megget Reservoir, 16
Meldons, 68
Memorial Hospital, Tweed Green, 12, 20, 65-7
Miller family, 60
milk cart, 38, 109
milking, milking machine, 44, 47-8
mill horn, 52
mills, mill workers, 13-4, 21, 52-5, 62, 72, 123
Ministers', Minnies', Pool, 7, 87
Mission Hall, 72-4
Montgomery Place, 35
Moray House, Edinburgh, 46, 102
Morelands Nursing Home, 20, 65
music, 68-70

Neal, Bill, travelling shop, 121
Neidpath Castle, 7, 30, 37, 39, 58, 77-8, 92
Neidpath Inn, 35-6
Nelson, Nellie, 120
Newby, 26, 40
North Street, 72
Northgate, 13, 51, 61, 63, 66, 79, 109, 121-2

O'Hara, Mr, teacher, 28
oil lamps, 15, 44-5
Old Parish Church, 53-4, 62, 72-7, 83-5, 89
Old Town, 9, 64, 66, 82, 114-5, 120-2

Parish Church, 53-4, 62, 72-7, 83-5, 89
Pathhead, 64
Paton, Dr. A., 63, 65-6
Peebles High School, 25-30, 36, 61, 70, 78, 111
Peeblesshire Advertiser, 56
Peeblesshire News, 63, 96, 123n
Penicuik, 60, 110-1
Peyton, Miss, matron of Manor Valley Sanatorium, 81
piping, 70
playground games, 26
plastering, plasterers, 10, 58, 60
Playhouse Cinema, 69
plumbers, 14, 62
poachers, poaching, 7, 9-11, 92
police, 10, 34, 92
Polish troops, 98-9, 101-3
pony and trap, 36, 40-1, 107
Poorhouse, 63
Port Brae, 14
Portobello, 107, 110-1
Post Office, 30, 56, 121
postman, 10
potatoes, 49-50
Priorsford School, 28

quarry, 32
Queen Elizabeth, 83
　　　Elizabeth II, 87
　　　Victoria, 71, 87
Queens, Beltane, 30, 74-9, 82

railway, 12, 72, 109-13
Railway Mission, 72-4
raspberries, 34
reaper-binder, 45
Red Lion House, 24
Renwick's, grocers, 20, 114-5, 122
Robson, Willie, 69
roller-skating, 68
Rosetta Road, 18, 30, 37, 79, 120
Royal Artillery, 100
Royal Scots, 99, 104
Russell family, 43

St. Andrew's Church, 72-3, 89, 116
St. Joseph's School, 28
St. Peter's Episcopal Church, 72, 84
salmon, 7, 10-1
Salvation Army, 72
sand, sand boat, 58-60
Sand Bridge, 73, 111
Sanderson's, chemist, 63
school bell, 26
School Brae, 14
schools, 25-30
Scotsman The, 38, 96
Scott bros, ironmongers 116
Scott family, 69
Scott, John, sweet and wool shop, 121
Scott, Pym, grocer, 117
Scott, Sir Robert, Lord Lieutenant of Peeblesshire, 86-7
Scott, Sir Walter, 7
Second World War, 28, 44, 66-7, 79, 90, 98-105, 118
Shaw, Brian, lawyer, Town Clerk of Innerleithen, 93
sheep, 35-7, 40-3, 45-7
sheep shearing, 47
shepherds, 35, 41, 43, 47, 114
Sheriff Court, 91-2
Sheriff family, 11
Shiel, Miss, teacher, 27
shops, 22, 114-123
Sinclair, Isabel, Sheriff, 11, 85, 93
skating, 14, 68
Skelton, tailors, 115, 121
Smith, John Ramsay
snow, 14-17, 44
Soonhope Glen, 32
South Park, 35, 38
spinning, 53
Sprot, Colonel A., 43, 77, 85
stations, 54, 110-3
Stevenson, Rob, general stores, 120
Stewart, Dr. H., 63-4, 66
Stobo, 29, 64
Stockie-In, 30, 33
stooks, 42
stourie-fit, 18
strawberry picking, 33
Sunday School, 72, 74
Sutherland, Miss, teacher, 28
swimming, 7, 33

tailor, 115
tartan, 52
teaching, teachers, 25-7, 56, 61
telegrams, 56
Temple, Dr., 65-6
tennis, 22, 30, 68-9, 72, 106
Thom, Dr., 66
Thorburn, Sir Michael, 53

Thorburn's Mills (Tweedside and Damdale), 13, 52-4
threshing, thrashing, 42, 44, 46
timber, 51, 56
Tinkerbell, 16
Toni's café, 70
Tontine, The, 63, 86, 93, 121
Town Clerks, 82-3, 93, 116
trains, 46-7, 90, 106-7, 109-112
travelling shops, 115, 121
trout, 8-9
Turnbull, Miss, teacher, 29
turnips, 42, 50
tweed, 52-3, 55
Tweed, river, 7-17, 58-9
Tweed Avenue, 13, 114
Tweed Brae, 14
Tweed Bridge, 7, 35, 66
Tweed Green, 8, 12-3, 18, 20, 23-4, 67, 89
Tweeddale Garage, 81, 102, 112
Tweeddale, Miss, teacher 28
Tweeddale Society, 71, 83, 108
Tweedsmuir, 35
Tweedsmuir, 1st Lord, see Buchan, John
    2nd Lord, 82
    Lady, 82

Upper Kidston, 26n, 27
Urquart, Harry, chemist, 63

Venlaw, 30, 32, 34, 102
Venlaw Castle, 68, 88
Victoria Park, 47, 69, 77, 101

wages, 46
walking, walks, 12, 68, 70
Warden of Cross Kirk, 77-8, 89
Warden of Neidpath, 77-8, 82
War Memorial, 60
washing day, 21, 28
water wheel, 44, 48
Watson family, 36-7
Weatherson, Peggy, 68
weaving, 52-5
weddings, 84
Wemyss, Earl of, 7, 38, 58
West Linton, 35, 61, 70, 87
Wetherston, saddlers, 1119
Wharton, Edith, 68
Whitebridge, Whitebrig, 7, 23, 34, 38
Wilson, Dr. and Dr. Robin, 63-6
Wilson, J. M., sheepdog trainer, 91
Wilson & Simes, restaurant
Wire Bridge and Cottage, 11-2
Women's Guild, 72, 84

yarn, 53-4
Young, Robert, watchmaker, 61
Young Street